REFUGEES
Human rights
have no borders

Amnesty International Publications

Amnesty International is a worldwide voluntary movement that works to prevent some of the gravest violations by governments of people's fundamental human rights. The main focus of its campaigning is to:
— *free all prisoners of conscience.* These are people detained anywhere for their beliefs or because of their ethnic origin, sex, colour, language, national or social origin, economic status, birth or other status — who have not used or advocated violence;
— *ensure fair and prompt trials for political prisoners;*
— *abolish the death penalty, torture and other cruel treatment of prisoners;*
— *end extrajudicial executions and "disappearances".*

Amnesty International also opposes abuses by opposition groups: hostage-taking, torture and killings of prisoners and other deliberate and arbitrary killings.

Amnesty International, recognizing that human rights are indivisible and interdependent, works to promote all the human rights enshrined in the Universal Declaration of Human Rights and other international standards, through human rights education programs and campaigning for ratification of human rights treaties.

Amnesty International is impartial. It is independent of any government, political persuasion or religious creed. It does not support or oppose any government or political system, nor does it support or oppose the views of the victims whose rights it seeks to protect. It is concerned solely with the protection of the human rights involved in each case, regardless of the ideology of the government or opposition forces, or the beliefs of the individual.

Amnesty International does not grade countries according to their record on human rights; instead of attempting comparisons it concentrates on trying to end the specific violations of human rights in each case.

Amnesty International has around 1,000,000 members and subscribers in 162 countries and territories. There are 4,273 local Amnesty International groups registered with the International Secretariat and several thousand school, university, professional and other groups in 80 countries in Africa, the Americas, Asia, Europe and the Middle East. To ensure impartiality, each group works on cases and campaigns in countries other than its own, selected for geographical and political diversity. Research into human rights violations and individual victims is conducted by the International Secretariat of Amnesty International. No section, group or member is expected to provide information on their own country, and no section, group or member has any responsibility for action taken or statements issued by the international organization concerning their own country.

Amnesty International has formal relations with the United Nations Economic and Social Council (ECOSOC); the United Nations Educational, Scientific and Cultural Organization (UNESCO); the Council of Europe; the Organization of American States; the Organization of African Unity; and the Inter-Parliamentary Union.

Amnesty International is financed by subscriptions and donations from its worldwide membership. No funds are sought or accepted from governments. To safeguard the independence of the organization, all contributions are strictly controlled by guidelines laid down by the International Council.

REFUGEES
Human rights
have no borders

Amnesty International Publications
1 Easton Street, London WC1X 8DJ
United Kingdom

First published 1997
by Amnesty International Publications
1 Easton Street, London WC1X 8DJ, United Kingdom

AI Index: ACT 34/03/97
ISBN: 0 86210 265 0
Original language English

Printed by: Alden Press, Osney Mead,
Oxford OX2 0EF, United Kingdom

Cover design: John Finn, Artworkers

Cover photograph: Tajiki refugee woman in Afghanistan
© Roger Job/Gamma/Frank Spooner

CONTENTS

Preface

Amnesty International's one million members around the world believe that human rights are for everyone. They lobby governments all over the world to improve their human rights records and to use their influence over other states to enhance the protection of human rights. Amnesty International's members work with the news media to expose abuses and mobilize public opinion. They organize locally, nationally and internationally to build the momentum for change. They collaborate with other organizations, including refugee groups, in the struggle to build a fairer and safer world.

As part of this work, Amnesty International opposes the forcible return (*refoulement*) of any person to a country where he or she would be at risk of falling victim to imprisonment as a prisoner of conscience[1], torture, "disappearance", extrajudicial execution or the death penalty. This is the basis of Amnesty International's work for refugees. It is an important element of preventive human rights work — acting to prevent human rights violations, not just responding after they have occurred. Amnesty International calls on governments to ensure that they do not obstruct asylum-seekers' access to their countries and that they provide asylum procedures that are fair, impartial and thorough. The organization demands that no asylum-seeker is forcibly expelled without having had his or her claim properly examined. It also calls on states to ensure that they do not expel anyone to a country which may itself forcibly return them to danger.

Much of Amnesty International's work on behalf of refugees is carried out by the movement's national sections based in the countries where people seek protection. Amnesty International members provide information about human rights violations in asylum-seekers' countries of origin to governments, to those who make decisions on asylum claims, and to lawyers and others working on behalf of asylum-seekers. Amnesty International's sections also monitor governments' asylum policies and practices to ensure they are adequate to identify and protect those at risk. In some cases,

Amnesty International members intervene directly with the authorities to prevent the *refoulement* of a refugee.

This report is part of a worldwide Amnesty International campaign for refugees' human rights. The campaign, launched in March 1997, focuses on three cornerstone issues, which are increasingly threatened, undermined or ignored by governments around the world:

- human rights protection in countries of origin — action to prevent human rights violations, so that people are not forced to leave their countries in search of safety;
- human rights protection in countries of asylum — action to ensure that those who flee human rights violations are allowed to reach a place of safety, that they are given effective protection against *refoulement*, and that their human rights are respected in their host country;
- human rights protection at the international level — action to ensure that human rights considerations are paramount in decisions about refugee protection issues, such as the need for protection of people internally displaced within their own countries, developments in international refugee law and practice, and programs for refugees to return home.

Human rights activists involved with refugees face a dual challenge at the international level. They must defend the protection provided by international refugee and human rights law in the face of growing government efforts to avoid and circumvent their obligations. They must also strive to ensure that as new human rights challenges arise, the system of international protection is able to meet those challenges.

Amnesty International urges all people concerned with human rights to join this campaign to remind the world's governments that every refugee is a human being with rights that must be respected.

Introduction

"People often ask what it was like, but most people don't listen when you tell them how bad it really was."
A Bosnian woman refugee

Refugees have been forced to abandon their homes, friends and livelihoods. Some have responded instinctively to an immediate and terrible threat. Others have taken the painful decision to leave their country after a long period of uncertainty, when all other options have failed. All have had their lives overturned by forces beyond their control. Each would be at grave risk of human rights violations if returned home.

Every refugee is entitled to international protection. But the international system that is supposed to protect refugees is in crisis. Over recent years the number of refugees has significantly increased — from around eight million a decade ago to around 15 million today — as human rights crises have proliferated. At the same time, governments' commitment to offering asylum is dwindling, as is their political will to resolve the crises from which people have been forced to flee.

This report shows that there is a clearly identifiable (and preventable) reason for the flight of so many refugees from their homes — human rights violations. Some such people who have fled from their countries have been given asylum. Others have not. This report explains how international and regional refugee treaties define who is eligible for protection as a refugee, and what rights refugees are entitled to under these treaties. It emphasizes that refugees are entitled to have all their basic human rights protected.

The report highlights the ways in which governments are evading or avoiding their international obligations towards refugees. It addresses refugee issues that are currently being debated by the international community, including voluntary repatriation, "temporary protection" and the failure of governments to share the responsibility for the world's refugees. The report concludes by making a series of recommendations based on human rights principles to ensure protection for refugees.

Amnesty International believes such steps are urgently needed to safeguard the interests of the 15 million individuals who have uprooted themselves to search for safety. The overwhelming majority of these people — 90 per cent — live in the south, many in the world's poorest countries. Africa shelters more than twice as many refugees as Europe, North America and Oceania combined. This stark fact reflects the sad reality that northern states, despite their small share of the world's refugee population, have taken concerted steps to make it nearly impossible for refugees to enter their territories and to deny protection to many of those who do succeed.

The cases highlighted in this report reflect only a small proportion of the world's refugees. Typically, refugees have walked across a border to a neighbouring country, where they eke out a precarious living or depend on often unreliable relief supplies. The vast majority are women and children, a reality often hidden by the fact that most of those who manage to reach relatively wealthy countries and apply for asylum are men. Most women have fled for the same reasons as men — to avoid repression, violence and human rights abuses. Some, however, have left their countries to escape abuses that are directed solely or primarily at women, such as sexual violence. Some women seek sanctuary abroad from "private" violence, such as domestic violence, when their government will make no effort to protect them, or to avoid female genital mutilation. Other women, as well as men, face persecution because of their sexual orientation.

In addition to the world's 15 million refugees, an estimated 25 to 30 million people have been forced to leave their homes because of human rights violations or threats to their lives, but have not crossed — or have been unable to cross — an international border. They are displaced within their own countries. Again, most are in the poorest parts of the world, often within or near conflict zones. The international response to the plight of internally displaced people has been uneven at best, and at worst driven by narrow political and economic interests.

Continuing human rights violations

The human rights violations that force people to seek international protection continue unabated. All over the world, governments driven by political expediency and self-interest commit atrocities.

"To leave any of the independent republics of the former Soviet Union is practically impossible for someone who has been involved in opposition political activity."

Shokhrat Kadyrov emerged from a bureaucratic nightmare in July 1996. For two nerve-racking months he had been trapped in Moscow, despite having papers granting him refugee status in Norway.

A 42-year-old writer and journalist from Turkmenistan, he became active in the country's political opposition in 1991, helping to establish an informal weekly political discussion club known as *Paykhas*. Later that year he was detained by the police for questioning, and the *Paykhas* club was banned. In 1992 he was twice put under effective house arrest, once to prevent him from attending a human rights conference in Kyrgyzstan. The following year he was refused permission to travel abroad. Throughout, he believed he was under constant surveillance by state officials.

In August 1993 Shokhrat left Turkmenistan with his wife, Larisa, and 15-year-old son, Kirill, to become refugees in Moscow (they had no residency rights there). He subsequently heard that Turkmen officials had approached the Russian authorities seeking his extradition, as they had done with other Turkmen political exiles. He then began the search to find asylum further afield.

Finally, in May 1996, Norway offered the family entry and work permits as refugees, and asked the Moscow authorities to issue them emergency travel documents. Weeks went by and nothing happened. After much lobbying by Amnesty International and others, the family eventually received the required exit permission. They have now settled safely in Norway and are looking forward to their new life.

They stand by while police officers and prison guards torture prisoners. They actively or tacitly encourage their forces to kill political opponents or people identified as "undesirable". They foster ethnic division and racial violence. Some states have disintegrated into a patchwork of territories controlled by warring factions for whom looting, raping and killing have become routine. Vicious internal conflicts, often based on ethnic differences, have spread. And so individuals, families and whole communities are forced to seek refuge abroad.

Every refugee has a unique story to tell — a story of repression and abuse, of fear and flight. If governments fulfilled their responsibilities — if they protected their citizens instead of persecuting them — then millions of women, men and children would not have to gamble on an uncertain future in a foreign land, and those in exile could return home safely.

The growing number of refugees is neither a temporary problem nor the random product of chance events. It is the predictable consequence of human rights crises, the result of decisions made by individuals who wield power over people's lives. Amnesty International calls on states to learn from past mistakes and to heed the warnings of human rights organizations. In the past those warnings have too often been ignored with tragic consequences. In the year before the outbreak of genocidal violence in Rwanda, the UN was repeatedly urged by human rights organizations, as well as its own senior advisers, to take action to protect civilians from massacres. These appeals were not heeded. The UN's member states allowed the situation to deteriorate and then, when mass killings began, withdrew almost all UN troops. More than two million Rwandese refugees fled their country.

Refugees are not necessarily safe even when they have succeeded in escaping. Some continue to be at risk of violence, either from their own nationals or from the security forces or citizens of the country of asylum. Some are confined to areas close to the border, leaving them vulnerable to cross-border attacks. Sometimes refugee camps are effectively controlled by exiles who committed massive human rights violations in their country of origin and have not been brought to justice. Often refugees are in countries whose governments have a record of abusing the human rights of their own citizens, and behave no better towards refugees. Many refugees have been murdered and mutilated in the very place they had fled to for safety. Women and girls are particularly at risk of sexual violence. They are vulnerable during flight, when they may be attacked by pirates, bandits, border guards, members of the security forces, local residents or other refugees. Women confined in refugee camps, sometimes for years, are at risk of rape, assault and exploitation by officials and other refugees.

A declining commitment to refugees

Many governments pay lip service to the rights of refugees while in practice devoting their energies to keeping refugees away from their borders, so that they do not have to honour their obligations. Some states that have traditionally hosted large numbers of refugees now turn them away because of the international community's failure to share the responsibility for protecting refugees. In many countries, officials apply a restrictive interpretation of who should qualify for protection as refugees under the main international refugee treaty, the 1951 UN Convention relating to the Status of Refugees (the UN Refugee Convention) and its 1967 Protocol, with the result that people fleeing persecution are returned to their persecutors.

Fundamental to the protection of refugees is the principle of *non-refoulement*— that no one should be forcibly returned to a country where his or her life or freedom would be at risk. This principle is spelled out in Article 33 of the UN Refugee Convention and in international human rights law. The principle is so widely accepted that it is generally regarded as binding on all states, whether or not they have signed the international refugee treaties. Despite this, many countries are forcing men, women and children back to their persecutors. Every time the principle of *non-refoulement* is breached, someone's life or freedom is deliberately endangered.

One of the main ways governments are trying to avoid their obligations to refugees is by physically preventing asylum-seekers from entering their country. Alone, or in regional groups, they are fortifying their borders. They impose visa requirements that are in practice impossible for asylum-seekers to fulfil. They fine airlines and shipping companies if they allow people without the necessary paperwork to board their craft. Asylum-seekers find themselves denied a route to safety by airline or shipping staff, as well as by immigration officials.

"They stripped me naked and assaulted me. I begged them to kill me. Instead, they cut off my hands with machetes."

Sallay Goba was stripped naked and sexually assaulted. She begged the men in uniform to kill her, but they ignored her pleas. Instead they cut off both her hands with machetes. They tied her hands to her elbows with string and told her to take this "message" to the nearby town of Bo, in the Southern Province of Sierra Leone.

Sallay Goba, a woman in her fifties, had already lost her husband, her son-in-law and three of her grandchildren. They were killed in a rebel attack in 1994 in Eastern Province. After her family was killed she fled for safety to Mattru, near Bo. But in October 1995 an armed group attacked Mattru.

After her mutilation, it took Sallay three days to reach Bo. During the following weeks and months thousands more people arrived in Bo seeking help after attacks on their villages in the surrounding countryside. Men, women and children arrived with their fingers, hands and arms deliberately severed by their attackers. Others had been sexually assaulted, slashed with machetes or shot. The identity of those responsible was often unclear: both government soldiers and rebels, who wore the same uniforms and carried the same weapons, were implicated in attacks. By mid-1996 some 230,000 people who had lost their homes, possessions and livelihoods had sought refuge in Bo.

The armed conflict in Sierra Leone, which began in 1991, has exacted an appalling toll on the people of Sierra Leone. Unarmed civilians have suffered atrocities such as torture and killings committed by both government forces and an armed opposition group, the Revolutionary United Front (RUF). According to UN estimates in 1996, more than two million people — nearly half the country's population — had been forced to leave their homes as a result of the conflict. Over 350,000 crossed into neighbouring Guinea and Liberia and became refugees. The rest remained internally displaced within Sierra Leone.

Desperate families are not even given a chance to put their case for asylum. The seas are patrolled and boats are prevented from docking. Borders are closed, and troops ensure that no one crosses. All these measures — dubbed mechanisms of *non-entrée* — prevent refugees from exercising their right to seek asylum.[2]

Some states off-load their obligations by sending asylum-seekers to a "safe third country". Usually this is a country that an asylum-seeker has travelled through, although sometimes it is simply where the person has had to change planes. Often the third country is far from safe, and will not provide protection. Some of the countries considered "safe" by states turning away asylum-seekers have not ratified and implemented the international refugee treaties, let alone established procedures for dealing properly with asylum-seekers.

One of the most cruel ironies is that people fleeing persecution — many of whom have been detained and tortured at home — are sometimes imprisoned when they do manage to enter a "safe" country. According to international law, asylum-seekers should not be detained unless they have been charged with a criminal offence, or the detention is necessary and allowed under international standards. Yet some states continue to use detention as a means to deter refugees from seeking asylum or to encourage them to abandon their asylum application.

Those refugees who do gain access to countries where they apply for asylum face procedures that vary enormously from state to state and often fall below international standards. In some countries decisions on asylum cases are effectively made by a lone immigration official, acting without any human rights or legal advice. Sometimes proceedings are carried out in a language the asylum-seeker does not understand, without an interpreter. Life and death decisions are often made in one or two hours. The principles that should guarantee a fair and satisfactory asylum procedure are neither complex nor demanding: any government that claims to uphold international refugee law should comply with them.

The economic and political interests that led states in the north to accept refugees willingly in the years after the Second World War have receded, while the number of people needing international protection has increased in recent years. Many governments have pandered to anti-immigrant rhetoric to justify

restricting the protection they offer to refugees. The proportion of
asylum claims which are accepted has plummeted as decision-
makers apply increasingly restrictive practices and interpretations
of the UN Refugee Convention, encouraging allegations that the
asylum system is being abused by "undeserving" claimants. Politi-
cians have used the high rejection rates to argue that the majority of
asylum-seekers are not genuine refugees but economic migrants,
seeking to bypass immigration controls in search of a higher standard of living. Political leaders have failed to educate the public
about international obligations towards refugees, and have not
challenged the perception that migrants are a major cause of
economic and social problems. The result has been violent hate
campaigns against refugees in some countries, and more and more
human tragedies, as people genuinely at risk of political imprisonment, torture and death are sent back to a horrific fate.

International responses

The international body with statutory responsibility for refugees is
the Office of the UN High Commissioner for Refugees (UNHCR),
whose work is overseen by the Executive Committee of UNHCR
(EXCOM— see Appendix II). UNHCR's mandate is primarily to
protect and assist refugees and "people of concern" to UNHCR,
and to seek permanent solutions to their problems. Many critics of
UNHCR say that it has wavered from its focus on protecting
refugees by working to a new agenda based on "humanitarian
action". According to its statute, UNHCR is non-political, yet it
operates in a political environment as it struggles to persuade states
to respond to refugee movements. It is funded by states on a year-to-
year basis and is effectively dependent on government approval of
its operations, so it is often unable to exert effective pressure on
governments that violate their international obligations towards
refugees. In some situations, it has refrained from criticizing countries whose actions are undermining the international system of
refugee protection, thereby appearing to be equivocal about the
authority of international refugee law.

    The international system of refugee protection has been put
under the greatest strain when mass flows of desperate people have
crossed borders, often within a short space of time, and have not
been able to return home for long periods. Some governments

have argued that they can no longer host large numbers of refugees because the refugees pose a threat to their national security. Some have said that they can no longer sustain the economic or environmental costs.

Governments can only be expected to provide sanctuary to hundreds of thousands of refugees if there is an effort by the international community both to resolve the situation in the country of origin so that the refugees can return in safety and to share fairly the costs of protection in the interim. Experience shows, however, that restoring an environment to which people can return safely is extremely difficult and requires enormous and sustained international effort. The international community has to combine providing long-term protection and assistance to large refugee populations with finding ways to restore respect for human rights in the country from which the refugees have fled.

The duty of states not to return a person to a situation where their life or freedom are at risk is absolute. What is less clear is how much discretion states have to qualify the nature of the protection they offer contingent on promises of international support or international efforts to resolve the initial human rights crisis.

One growing trend is for states to grant refugees "temporary protection" on a group basis rather than refugee status in their own right. This denies them access to individual asylum procedures and to the full set of rights associated with refugee protection. What was intended as a temporary measure has for many refugees meant years of living in limbo, with few rights and seemingly endless uncertainty about their future. It also leaves them vulnerable to being sent home as part of a group to situations where some individuals may face persecution.

In the past few years, new forms of international response have emerged, prompting a widespread belief that international and national obligations towards refugees are being redefined. One such response has been to contain potential refugees within their home countries using devices such as the "safe havens" and humanitarian areas which were established in Iraq and former Yugoslavia. In the short term, such solutions may have offered people at grave risk some respite. However, the interventions were inextricably linked to border closures that left no escape route for people who would flee if they could. Furthermore, the safety of the

"People in Algeria are killed and slaughtered without any reason at all... Some people are killed because their names were mentioned in a list; others because their names were omitted from another list... Both the government and the Islamists are killing innocent people... The international community has so far remained indifferent to what is happening in Algeria."

An Algerian wrote this letter to Amnesty International in 1996 in a desperate attempt to highlight the political violence in Algeria that has resulted in more than 50,000 killings since 1992. Many of the victims have died in armed confrontations between security forces and armed opposition groups. But as the violence has spiralled out of control, civilians have increasingly borne the brunt of the carnage.

The security forces have extrajudicially executed people in the street, in their homes and in detention centres. Hundreds of people have "disappeared" after arrest by military security and police. Torture and ill-treatment are routine. At the same time armed groups defining themselves as "Islamic" have murdered civilians and committed other grave abuses, including rape. All over the country, people are living in constant fear they may be next on the list. Women are particularly afraid, as they are targeted by one side for not wearing the veil, and by the other for wearing the veil.

The Algerian Government has proved incapable of protecting its citizens. As a result, thousands have made the painful decision to flee abroad to seek asylum. Sadly, many find that even that choice is closed to them or leads to further uncertainty and danger.

Those who try to reach Western Europe are often blocked by governments that have adopted entirely contradictory positions. On the one hand the governments have warned their own citizens to leave Algeria or not to visit the country because their security cannot be guaranteed by the Algerian authorities. On the other hand, they have refused to acknowledge that Algerian refugees have fled for their lives and would be in danger if returned.

Several Western European embassies in Algeria no longer issue visas and many others require guarantees that applicants will be returning to Algeria. Refugees who do manage to reach Europe are increasingly being denied asylum. Those fleeing persecution by armed groups have been told by receiving states that there is no evidence that their persecution is encouraged or tolerated by the authorities and that therefore their cases fall outside the UN Refugee Convention, which is not the case (see Chapter 3). There is ample evidence, however, that this is untrue. Asylum-seekers fleeing persecution by the security forces face similar reasons for rejection.

Some Algerian asylum-seekers, such as members of the judiciary, fall into both categories. If they do their job they risk being killed by armed groups. If they refuse to work, they risk punishment by the authorities. Just one example was the case of Ali,* a magistrate. In the course of his work he had to judge cases of individuals accused of "terrorism". After he had the courage to order medical examinations of detainees who he said had been tortured so badly they could not speak, the authorities transferred him to a Special Court in a region known as a stronghold of armed Islamist groups. He knew his life was in danger. His fears intensified after a magistrate was killed and several were threatened with death. Finally he decided the risks were too great and fled to France.

Instead of welcoming him, the French Office for the Protection of Refugees and the appeal court dismissed his claim for asylum. He was then told he had to go back to Algeria within a month. After much lobbying by human rights groups, the French authorities in May 1996 gave him

A bomb explosion in a residential area east of Algiers in 1995 which killed at least six people.
© Associated Press

temporary permission to stay for one year
under "*asile territorial*", rather than offering him refugee status. This means his
wife and child will find it virtually impossible to join him in France. Under French
procedures, his leave to stay should be
renewed until it is safe for him to return to
Algeria. Ali has no guarantees, however.
He still lives with uncertainty and fear, a
victim of unfair asylum procedures that
have blighted the lives of thousands of
Algerians and other nationals fleeing to
France in search of safety.
   * pseudonym

havens could not be guaranteed, with tragic results for thousands of women, men and children from Bosnia and Iraq.

Some governments argue that emphasis should be placed on "the right to remain", pointing out that the international protection provided to refugees by countries of asylum cannot replace the protection that people should receive from their own government. Clearly, no one should have to go into exile to find security. If the new approaches meant that more concerted efforts were made to improve the human rights situation in countries marked by abuses, this would be a step forward. However, the evidence suggests that the "right to remain" is being used by states to justify closing borders and confining would-be refugees in dangerous situations. This violates a general principle of international refugee law, enshrined in the Universal Declaration of Human Rights (UDHR), that everyone has the right to seek and to enjoy asylum from persecution. It also has an all too evident human cost.

Other methods are also being used to facilitate the early return of refugees, including the deployment of UN human rights monitors in Cambodia, Haiti and Rwanda; the establishment of *ad hoc* war crimes tribunals for former Yugoslavia and Rwanda; and a renewed emphasis on voluntary repatriation schemes, whether truly voluntary or not.[3]

Governments and UNHCR are currently promoting voluntary repatriation as the favoured solution to refugee problems. UNHCR's emphasis on this approach appears to be a pragmatic attempt, in the face of continued pressure from governments, to halt the erosion of refugee protection by ensuring the early return of refugees to their homes. However, the reality for many refugees has been return home under "voluntary repatriations" that are not truly voluntary and before conditions are sufficiently and durably safe. By comparison, there is remarkably little attention paid to the other "durable" solutions of integration in the country of asylum or resettlement in a third country.

All of these practices — obstructing access to their countries, applying asylum criteria restrictively, detaining asylum-seekers or containing, temporarily protecting or "voluntarily" repatriating refugees — show that states are not responding to refugee crises in ways that respect the basic human rights of refugees.

1 Refugees: fear, flight and further suffering

Five armed men surrounded Pascal Murwirano, a 22-year-old Rwandese refugee, in November 1996. He had sought shelter in an orphanage in eastern Zaire, hoping to avoid the conflict sweeping the area.

"'Are you from Rwanda?'

'Yes.'

'Are you Hutu?'

'Yes.'

'Take off your clothes.'

"Pascal crossed himself. He unbuttoned the first button of his shirt and before he could unbutton the second one, he was shot. He took one bullet in the heart, four in the stomach and one in the head."

This eye-witness account came from a Zairian refugee, one of thousands who fled into Tanzania in late 1996 in fear of their lives. All over the world people become refugees because of fear. Fear of human rights violations. Fear of random violence. Fear of persecution.

Human rights and refugees are not separate issues. If governments protected human rights there would be no refugees.

There were hopes at the beginning of the 1990s that the end of the Cold War would bring greater respect for human rights. There were expectations of international collaboration in pursuit of peace, human rights and development, and an end to proxy wars fought out in other people's countries. The reality has been very different. Millions of people have had their lives shattered by wars, secessionist conflicts and sectarian violence. Many others have suffered state repression, ethnic hatred, religious intolerance or gender-based persecution. In desperation, they have chosen the only option left to them — leave their homes in search of safety.

This chapter explores some of the reasons behind the flight of refugees. It is based on Amnesty International's core work —

researching and exposing the human rights violations covered by its mandate. It cannot be exhaustive: every refugee has a unique experience of fear and flight and the underlying reasons for persecution are numerous. What is clear is that refugee crises can only be resolved if the underlying human rights issues are addressed.

Since the early 1970s the causes for flight have included: the aftermath of the end of colonial rule; the partition of states; struggles for autonomy; political violence and repression; ethnic and religious struggles, sometimes leading to genocide; "ethnic cleansing"; discrimination; and armed conflict. The resulting human rights violations, either committed by governments or not prevented by them, have meant that large-scale population movements have touched every continent in the world.

Armed conflicts

In the 1990s Europe witnessed its worst human rights disaster since the 1940s. As the former Yugoslavia disintegrated, forcible expulsion, mass murder and rape became regular occurrences. A refugee from former Yugoslavia told Amnesty International:

> "Everybody slaughters whom he chooses and where he chooses. Total freedom of slaughter and harassment... nobody is responsible for anything."

In Bosnia-Herzegovina alone, more than half the population was uprooted by the war, with an estimated 1.3 million people displaced inside the country. Around half a million Bosnian refugees went to other republics of the former Yugoslavia, where some faced further nationalist violence and the risk of *refoulement*. Many tried to go elsewhere in Europe, but failed because visa requirements were rapidly imposed by almost all European countries after the war had started. Most of the 600,000 who did reach Western Europe were granted "temporary protection" instead of access to a normal procedure that would determine whether they were in need of protection as refugees under the UN Refugee Convention.

In other parts of the world too there have been similarly tragic stories of states disintegrating under the pressure of internal conflict, often fuelled over many years by external powers. Such conflicts have involved systematic violence, with civilians caught in the middle, frequently targeted by both sides for vicious human rights abuses. They have meant the breakdown of state authority so there

Augusto Gomes survives by selling single cigarettes from a hut he made out of sticks and grass. Around him are countless more grass huts, constructed by people internally displaced in Angola in 1993 as a result of the civil war. The place is called Porto Quipiri, the temporary home for many of the 90,000 people who used to live in Nambuangongo, 145 kilometres north of the capital, Luanda.

Augusto fled with his parents and 12 brothers and sisters after forces belonging to UNITA, an armed opposition group, took control of his village in April 1993. He still finds it distressing to explain the carnage they escaped.

"UNITA hunted people in the bush. Those who were caught were brought to the village and killed. Some were shot. Others were axed with machetes. Some were cut up after they were shot. Some old people... were locked up in houses which were then set on fire."

For weeks Augusto's family and friends lived in the bush before slowly making their way by foot to Porto Quipiri, 50 kilometres from Luanda. Many became ill, with vomiting, diarrhoea and internal bleeding. At least 50 people died, mostly children and the elderly. Some of the dead could not be buried.

They first stopped at Caxito, where for two months they struggled to avoid starvation as no food aid was provided. Two hundred people died. When they eventually reached Porto Quipiri, they were given some rations, although barely enough to live on. In 1995 Augusto's wife died.

Augusto and his family want to return home when it is safe. They complain that many people in authority are aware of the appalling conditions they are suffering in the camp. But, Augusto says, "nobody does anything about it."

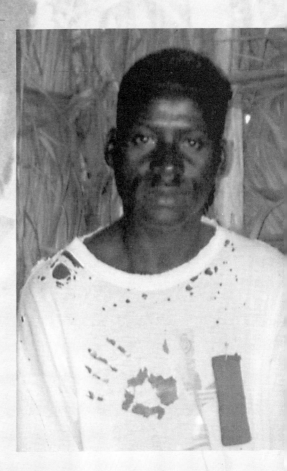

is no one to turn to for protection. They have meant survival has become a matter of luck, not of right — and that often the only chance of safety has been through flight. Among the countries most affected by such crises in recent years have been Afghanistan, Angola and Liberia, all of which have seen a large proportion of their population flee to other countries or displaced within their own country.

Many other states racked by internal conflict and the associated human rights abuses have seen vast numbers of people forced to flee abroad or to other parts of their country. These include Algeria, Burundi, Colombia, Sierra Leone, Somalia, Sri Lanka and Sudan.

In several parts of the world the brutal repression of national independence movements continues to cause people to flee. Among the victims are people from East Timor, fleeing Indonesian Government repression, and Tibetans, escaping religious and political persecution by the Chinese authorities. The war between the Russian Government and the secessionists of the Chechen Republic, which began in late 1994, saw Russian troops bombard the capital city, Grozny, until two-thirds of the houses had been destroyed. The majority of the city's population of 400,000 fled. Most went to stay with friends and relatives elsewhere in the Chechen Republic; others went to neighbouring autonomous republics within the Russian Federation.

War and repression of particular communities have combined to create refugee crises. During the Gulf War in 1990 to 1991, hundreds of thousands of people were expelled from or fled Kuwait and other Gulf states. In the aftermath of the war, an estimated two million Iraqi Kurds and Shi'a Muslims from southern Iraq escaped appalling levels of brutality by Iraqi forces, ending up in vast camps in Iran, Turkey and elsewhere. Such sudden mass movements of people always signal terror and human rights catastrophes.

Political repression

Every day in countries all over the world individuals make the agonizing decision to leave their homeland. They may be political activists who have discovered that the police are looking for them — and in their country suspected opponents of the government face torture or death. They may be members of a political, religious

The following equations appear on the blackboard:

$$41+29+3 =$$
$$106+2+34 =$$
$$74+40+37 =$$
$$28+3+415 =$$
$$34+910 =$$

Karenni refugee children from Myanmar in a camp on the Thai/Myanmar border.
© Howard J Davies

"I heard a soldier's voice and then I heard my [17-year-old] grand-daughter give a short but very loud scream, and then I heard her sobbing... The captain pulled her towards him and raped her. After he'd done so, he showed the girl his gun and said, 'No one is to know this event. If you tell anyone, I'll kill you'."

This family had already fled Myanmar (Burma) to escape persecution. The grandmother, a 54-year-old Mon Christian woman, described to Amnesty International how they had left the Pa Yaw refugee camp in Thailand and secretly crossed the border to collect two pigs from their village for a Christmas celebration. They were intercepted on the way back by 40 members of the Burmese army (the *tatmadaw*), who confiscated the pigs, interrogated them about opposition activity in the area, raped the young woman and threatened to kill them all. Eventually the family was allowed to return to the camp.

Such brutality has driven hundreds of thousands of Burmese people from their homes. Most are internally displaced, although many have sought sanctuary abroad. The worst affected are members of Myanmar's scores of ethnic and religious minorities, who make up a third of the population, particularly Karens (Kayin), Mons, Shan, Karennis and Rohingyas.

Gross human rights violations have continued unabated in Myanmar during the past eight years of military rule by the State Law and Order Restoration Council. Anyone who is a member of a minority group or who is suspected of opposition risks extrajudicial execution, imprisonment, torture and detention in inhuman conditions. Many people are forced to work for the state or military, during which they are tortured and ill-treated. An unknown number have died. In such a climate, many people feel they have no choice but to flee.

or human rights organization which has been targeted by the authorities. They may have received a death threat from an armed opposition group, and know their time is running out. All have a right to seek international protection, whether or not they are part of a mass exodus which has caught the world's attention.

Countless refugees have been forced to flee because of the ruthless determination of their rulers to hold on to power. The military government in Myanmar, which seized power in 1988, has brutally repressed the activities of the pro-democracy opposition. Its forces have killed and tortured thousands of people. Those most in danger are members of Myanmar's minority ethnic groups and those living in border areas where armed opposition groups are active. Untold numbers of women, men and children die or are tortured each year when forced to work as porters for the army. Hundreds of thousands of Burmese refugees have fled from this nightmare to neighbouring countries.

A strong indication of where human rights violations are endemic or persistent is the number of people fleeing a country. Governments may be able to restrict access to information. They may deny that any violations are occurring. But they can rarely stop desperate people escaping and then telling their stories.

The crammed boats bobbing precariously towards the USA from Haiti at various times over more than a decade exposed the brutality of successive Haitian governments. The steady flow of Iranians arriving at border points, ports and airports every year are living proof of the climate of fear in the country. Turkish Kurds seeking asylum abroad consistently describe the deliberate and systematic practice of torture, "disappearance" and extrajudicial execution by the Turkish authorities. The numbers of refugees from countries such as Chad and Togo show that the promises of greater respect for human rights made by new governments have been cruelly broken.

When large numbers of refugees belong to the same ethnic group, it usually means the group has been targeted for human rights abuses. Few people from northern Bhutan are refugees, while there are more than 90,000 refugees from southern Bhutan living in eastern Nepal. Most were forced to leave by the actions of the Bhutanese authorities in the early 1990s.

Refugees from Mali and Niger are almost all ethnic Tuaregs,

Two things used to dominate Gharib el-Arbi's life in Tunisia: the theatre and politics. Then something else took over. Fear.

In 1978, as a 19-year-old undergraduate studying the theatre, he joined an organization which later became *al-Nahda*, an Islamic opposition group. After leaving college he combined his two passions. With 10 others, he set up a theatre company which staged productions exploring cultural and political issues, often using political satire.

Gharib's fear began in 1982. He was arrested, deprived of his passport and imprisoned for six months for membership of *al-Nahda*. Two years later he was imprisoned again, this time for a year, and was tortured for 48 consecutive days. After his release, he continued to stage political plays, despite rising levels of repression against members of *al-Nahda*. Thousands of suspected *al-Nahda* members have been imprisoned after unfair trials, and reports of torture are received almost daily. Methods used include beatings on the soles of the feet, suspension by the ankles, electric shocks and the insertion of a bottle into the anus.

On the last day of 1993, Gharib realized his time was running out. Police poured into his theatre during a show and arrested four actors. He says one died in custody as a result of torture.

He managed to escape and went into hiding. After other friends and colleagues had been arrested, he decided he had no choice but to leave Tunisia and his beloved theatre company. In April 1994 he boarded a boat bound for Italy.

He now lives in a village near Como with two brothers. The Italian authorities have rejected his asylum claim and he is awaiting the outcome of an appeal. "I like Italy," he says, "but I would prefer to live in a country where the laws on refugees are respected."

who have fled government reprisals against Tuareg insurgents. Thousands of Oromos are still escaping from Ethiopia, despite general improvements in Ethiopia's human rights record.

There are other forms of persecution which fall outside Amnesty International's specific mandate that force people to flee their homes and become refugees. For example, discrimination can be so severe that it constitutes persecution. Victims of such persecution are entitled to protection.

Conditions after flight

The international refugee system should protect refugees as soon as they leave their country. The reality, however, is that many do not find the safety they deserve and are entitled to. Already traumatized by their experiences, they face new fears and new pain.

Many refugees, especially women, are abused during their flight in search of a sanctuary. Smugglers, border guards, pirates, members of armed groups, even other refugees, have all been known to abuse refugee women while they are in search of safety. Afghan women trying to reach Pakistan are frequently raped and tortured by members of armed groups and border guards. Vietnamese refugees on boats have been attacked by pirates and robbed, raped and killed. Convoys of refugees fleeing the Russian attack on the Chechen Republic have been deliberately sprayed with bullets and mortar shells.

The end of the flight does not necessarily mean the end of danger. Refugees living in camps are often dependent on rations that are distributed by groups responsible for abuses back home. The local power structure in the country of origin is often replicated — as are the abuses. Women in particular are vulnerable to rape or demands for "sexual favours" in exchange for food and water.

The camps are often in countries that are themselves racked by civil war or run by governments that flagrantly violate human rights. Refugee camps in eastern Zaire, for example, were heavily shelled by rebel forces in late 1996. Hundreds of unarmed refugees were killed. Hundreds of thousands were forced to abandon the camps.

Refugees can also find that their presence in a country is resented. The sudden arrival of large numbers of refugees can create real economic and environmental problems, and exacerbate existing political tensions. In these conditions, governments some-times offer them little or no protection, or actively contribute to an atmosphere in which refugees are attacked and abused by local people. This has sometimes been the case, for example, for Somalis in Kenya and for Afghans in Pakistan.

In several countries in the north, refugees have been victims of racist attacks by local people. They have had petrol bombs pushed through their doors or have been subjected to verbal and physical abuse as they walk in the street or attend school. In Germany, for example, African and Turkish refugees have been targeted for abuse and even burned to death in arson attacks on their homes.

In many places, however, refugees have overcome enormous obstacles to make the best of a bad situation. Generations of Pales-tinians living in camps in the Middle East have run schools, hospi-tals and workshops. Ethiopian and Eritrean refugees in camps in Sudan have organized income-generating schemes, such as raising chickens and dress-making, as well as literacy classes. In camps in Nepal, refugees from southern Bhutan run organizations that counsel victims of rape and teach basic skills. In some countries, refugees have been welcomed and integrated into communities and now play a full part in the life of their adopted countries.

In other cases, the dangers that drove refugees from their country have ended and people have been able to return home. Some do so as individuals, as did many of those who have returned to South Africa since the end of *apartheid*. Others return under repatriation schemes overseen by UNHCR or undertaken by gov-ernments working together. Almost 20,000 Guatemalan refugees returned from Mexico between 1993 and 1995, a process made pos-sible by an agreement reached with the Guatemalan Government. More than 1.7 million Mozambican refugees returned to their home areas from six neighbouring countries in two and a half years in the 1990s — the largest repatriation in African history.

However, the overwhelming majority of the world's refugees have little chance of an early return home in safety and dignity. They will continue to suffer abuses, dislocation and poverty while they wait for the world's governments to live up to their internation-al obligations to promote and respect human rights.

The Kurdish village of Ormanici in southeastern Turkey was largely evacuated following brutal security force operations in 1993. © Richard Wayman

Who is a refugee?

The internationally agreed definition of who is a refugee is spelled out in the 1951 UN Convention relating to the Status of Refugees (the UN Refugee Convention). This definition has been broadened in some regions by various regional agreements. In practice, there are significant differences in how states apply the relevant definition of who is entitled to protection as a refugee. This is influenced by how they view the causes of flight, which of these they recognize as forming a legitimate basis for granting protection, and in some cases by the political interests of host governments.

Amnesty International applies a simple standard in its work on refugees. Anyone who can reasonably be expected to be in danger of imprisonment as a prisoner of conscience, torture, execution or "disappearance" in their country should not be forced to return there.

In this report, when Amnesty International refers to refugees, the term includes all asylum-seekers fleeing persecution and human rights violations, including those who have not been formally recognized as refugees.

UN Refugee Convention

The UN Refugee Convention is an internationally agreed and legally binding treaty. It defines a refugee as a person who:

" ... owing to well-founded fear of being persecuted for reasons of race, religion, nationality, membership of a particular social group or political opinion, is outside the country of his nationality and is unable or, owing to such fear, is unwilling to avail himself of the protection of that country..."[4]

A person becomes a refugee as soon as he or she is in the situation defined in the UN Refugee Convention, not simply when another state has formally recognized his or her refugee status.

The "well-founded fear" in the UN Refugee Convention must be objectively measured. The standard of proof should favour the claimant. Generally, someone's fear of being persecuted is "well-founded" if it appears justified in light of the known facts about the country of origin and the particular circumstances of the individual.

"Persecution" is not defined in the Convention but has been interpreted in practice to mean a violation of someone's basic human rights of sufficient gravity that the protection of another state is needed.[5] The need for protection depends on the gravity of the harm and the type of human right involved.

The international community has decided that certain rights are so fundamental that they have to be respected at all times. A violation of any of these rights is considered to be persecution, whatever the circumstances. These rights, which are spelled out in the International Covenant on Civil and Political Rights (ICCPR), include:

● the right to life;

● the right to be protected from torture or cruel, inhuman or degrading treatment or punishment;

● the right not to be subjected to slavery or servitude;

● the right not to be subjected to prosecution for an act which did not constitute a criminal offence under law at the time when it was committed;

- the right to recognition as a person before the law;
- the right to freedom of thought, conscience and religion.

Attacks on other fundamental rights constitute persecution under international law unless the intensity of the attacks is particularly low. These rights, also covered by the ICCPR, include:

- liberty and security of the person, including freedom from arbitrary arrest and detention;
- liberty of opinion and expression;
- liberty of assembly and association;
- right to equal protection for all (which equals prohibition of discrimination);
- right to a fair and public hearing and to be presumed innocent unless guilt is proved;
- right to personal and family privacy and integrity;
- right to internal movement and choice of residence;
- freedom to leave and return to one's country.

OAU Convention

The Organization of African Unity (OAU) adopted in 1969 the OAU Convention, which is a binding treaty. It expanded the definition of refugees in Africa:

"The term 'refugee' shall also apply to every person who, owing to external aggression, occupation, foreign domination or events seriously disturbing public order in either part or the whole of his country of origin or nationality, is compelled to leave his place of habitual residence in order to seek refuge in another place outside his country of origin or nationality."[6]

Cartagena Declaration

In 1984, 10 Latin American states adopted the Cartagena Declaration, which also extended the definition of refugees in the Americas to:

"...persons who have fled their country because their lives, safety, or freedom have been threatened by generalized violence, foreign aggression, internal conflicts, massive violations of human rights or other circumstances which have seriously disturbed public order."[7]

Although the Cartagena Declaration is not legally binding, it has become the basis of refugee policy in the region and has been incorporated in the legislation of a number of states.

De facto refugees

There is general recognition that given the narrow definition of refugees within the UN Refugee Convention, an expanded class of "refugees" has a legitimate claim to some form of protection. UNHCR describes refugees and "people of concern" as those who have been forced to flee their country as a result of persecution, massive human rights violations, generalized violence, armed conflicts, civil strife or other circumstances that have seriously disturbed public order, threatening their lives, safety or freedom. Some of these people are protected as refugees; others are protected on humanitarian grounds as "non-refugees" who may face danger if returned to their country of origin. People who do not fit within the UN Refugee Convention's criteria or who have not been formally recognized as Convention refugees but cannot safely return to their country of origin are often called "de facto refugees".[8]

2 Refugees and human rights

The rights of refugees and basic human rights are inextricably linked. First, today's human rights abuses are tomorrow's refugee movements. Second, refugees are entitled to the same fundamental human rights as every other human being. The right to protection from *refoulement* that refugees have under international refugee law is simply another means by which basic human rights are safeguarded.

For historical reasons, people working on behalf of refugees and human rights groups have often appeared to pursue separate agendas. Yet the struggle for the rights of refugees is an integral part of the broader campaign for human rights, and international human rights standards provide authoritative tools and powerful mechanisms to support the protection of refugees.

Refugee protection is an important element in preventive human rights work; when every other safeguard fails, asylum in a foreign country is a direct and immediate method of human rights protection. The linkage between refugee rights and human rights can be seen in the fundamental principle of *non-refoulement*. This safeguard is the cornerstone of refugee law and is firmly established in international human rights treaties, such as the Convention against Torture and Other Cruel, Inhuman or Degrading Treatment or Punishment (Convention against Torture) and the ICCPR, both of which proscribe the return of a person to a place where they may be at risk of torture or cruel, inhuman or degrading treatment or punishment. Furthermore, the principle is generally considered to be a rule of international customary law — it is binding on all states, whether or not they have acceded to any of the treaties governing international refugee law and international human rights law.

The Universal Declaration of Human Rights (UDHR) sets out everyone's basic human rights. Article 14(1) states that "Everyone has the right to seek and to enjoy in other countries asylum from

Tamil refugees returned from India reunite with relatives and friends through the fence at Trincomalee reception centre, Sri Lanka.
© Howard J. Davies

persecution". This right was reiterated in the UN Declaration on Territorial Asylum, adopted by the UN General Assembly in 1967, although attempts to turn this into a binding treaty failed.[9] However, the general right to seek and to enjoy asylum does not constitute an individual right to be *granted* asylum: states have consistently shown great reluctance to agree international instruments that would impose duties on them to grant asylum.[10]

The UN Refugee Convention lays down minimum rights to which refugees are entitled, and obliges all states that have ratified the treaty to uphold them. It details types of refugee-specific rights, including *non-refoulement.* The Convention also covers basic civil rights for refugees as well as basic economic rights to enable refugees to provide for their own needs.

These rights should guarantee minimum standards for refugees within their country of asylum and should ensure that refugees are treated comparably in all states (according to their means) which are party to the UN Refugee Convention. However, these rights are increasingly being restricted, undermined or ignored.

Non-refoulement

Bouasria Ben Othman, an Algerian asylum-seeker, paid the ultimate price when the principle of *non-refoulement* was violated. On 15 July 1996 the Belgian authorities returned him to Algeria after refusing his asylum application, despite the clear risks he would face in his country. He immediately "disappeared". Four months later the Belgian authorities told Amnesty International that he had indeed been arrested on arrival in Algeria, then released, then rearrested in mid-November when trying to cross the border into Libya. On 26 November Bouasria appeared on Algerian television saying he was well and that people should stop asking about him. A week later Algerian police told his family that he had thrown himself out of a window while in detention and that he had died. He was 31 years old.

Non-refoulement is defined in Article 33(1) of the UN Refugee Convention:

> "No Contracting State shall expel or return ("*refouler*") a refugee in any manner whatsoever to the frontiers of territories where his life or freedom would be threatened on

account of his race, religion, nationality, membership of a particular social group or political opinion."

This principle applies to all refugees, including asylum-seekers whose status has not yet been determined and those seeking entry to a country.

Every person fleeing persecution and asking for asylum is protected by Article 33 from being rejected at a country's border. EXCOM has repeatedly stated that in all cases the "fundamental principle of *non-refoulement* including non-rejection at the frontier" must be ensured.[11] Sending anyone back who would be at risk of serious human rights violations or persecution in their home country constitutes a clear violation of the principle of *non-refoulement*, regardless of whether they have been allowed access to asylum procedures and even if their claim might have been refused.

Some refugees are not sent directly back to their country of origin, but are sent to another country which then sends them back without a fair and satisfactory assessment of their asylum claim. This constitutes indirect or chain *refoulement* and similarly contravenes the protection provided for under Article 33.

Refoulement is prohibited under Article 3 of the Convention against Torture. This provides that no one, including those convicted of crimes, should be sent back to a country where they would be at risk of torture. There are no exceptions to this provision.

Amnesty International consistently opposes the return of anyone to face the death penalty in all cases, including those involving war criminals. Host states can prosecute war criminals in their own countries — and if they do not have the appropriate laws, they should enact them.

An example of the successful use of such international human rights mechanisms is the case of Balabou Mutombo, a Zairian threatened with deportation from Switzerland. A member of an opposition party, he had been arrested in 1989 and tortured. Medical certificates confirmed his account. After his asylum application and appeal were rejected, his lawyer, supported by Amnesty International, took the case to the Committee Against Torture (a body set up under the Convention against Torture). The Committee examined his case and informed Switzerland that if Balabou Mutombo were returned to Zaire, this action would constitute a violation of Article 3 of the Convention against Torture. The Swiss

"I felt like someone going into space, I did not know what was going to happen to me."

Beatrice,* a 31-year-old refugee from Cameroon, was on a plane heading back home. She had tried to apply for asylum in Romania, but had been sent to Russia. She then sought asylum in Russia, but was marched onto a plane back to Cameroon.

Beatrice was involved with a political opposition party, the Social Democratic Front (SDF), and was detained several times between 1989 and 1996. After presidential elections in 1992, she says she was held for four days without food, questioned about her political activities and beaten with truncheons by two policemen.

In January 1996 she learned that the security forces were looking for her so she went into hiding. In March 1996 she escaped by plane to Romania, and tried to explain her position to immigration officials in Bucharest and to contact UNHCR:

"But when I got there the Romanian officials wouldn't listen to me. They did not grant me an interview at all. They put me back on the same plane that brought me to Moscow."

At Moscow airport she again tried to apply for asylum, but again officials ignored her pleas. "I asked for the number of UNHCR but they would not give it to me."

After a fortnight without news in Moscow airport's transit zone:

"Four men came up and said 'You're going, get ready.' They took my bag and walked with me to the plane. I tried to explain to them that it was dangerous for me to return, but they would not listen."

Beatrice arrived back in Cameroon and says she was immediately detained by the security forces but subsequently released after being made to sign a declaration that she would never participate in political activity. Using all the resources she had, she managed to escape again, this time leaving using a transit visa to Belarus, which then allowed her into the Russian Federation. Her current whereabouts and status are unknown.

* pseudonym

An airport in Russia © Trip

Government then annulled the deportation order.

The fundamental principle of *non-refoulement* is also contained in many other international human rights agreements, including Article 3 of the UN Declaration on Territorial Asylum; Article 8 of the UN Declaration on the Protection of All Persons from Enforced Disappearance; and Principle No. 5 of the UN Principles on the Effective Prevention and Investigation of Extra-legal, Arbitrary and Summary Executions. In addition, the Council of Europe told its member states in 1984 "that the principle of *non-refoulement* has been recognised as a general principle applicable to all persons", not just recognized refugees.[12]

There is also protection against *refoulement* in various regional human rights standards: the European Convention for the Protection of Human Rights and Fundamental Freedoms (ECHR); the American Convention on Human Rights; and the African Charter on Human and Peoples' Rights. The European Court of Human Rights, for example, referred to Article 3 of the ECHR when hearing the case of Karamjit Singh Chahal, a Sikh asylum-seeker in the UK.[13] He had been detained for more than six years facing possible deportation to India, where he would have been at risk of torture and other serious human rights violations. In November 1996 the European Court ruled that the protection offered by Article 3 is absolute and does not allow for any derogation. The Court instructed that Karamjit Singh Chahal should not be deported and that his detention should be subject to judicial scrutiny. He was immediately released.

The OAU Convention guarantees the principle of *non-refoulement*. The Cartagena Declaration stresses "the importance of the principle of non-return" and makes clear that this principle applies to all states, whether or not they are bound by a further treaty or agreement. Both the OAU Convention and the Cartagena Declaration explicitly identify rejection at the frontier as a breach of the *non-refoulement* principle.

The principle of *non-refoulement*, as laid down in the UN Refugee Convention, is not absolute. Article 33 states that it may be suspended if there are reasonable grounds for regarding the asylum-seeker as a danger to the security of the host country, or if the asylum-seeker has been convicted of "a particularly serious crime" and constitutes a danger to the host country.

Because of the fundamental importance of the principle of *non-refoulement*, the circumstances in which it may be suspended are very restricted. A state considering suspending the principle must ensure that the individual poses a clear danger to the public or to national security. It should take into account the proportionality of the sentence faced relative to the crime; the circumstances of the crime and other factors. For example, if a refugee who has been sentenced to one year's imprisonment for a public order offence is likely to face a further 30-year sentence if returned to his or her country of origin, then he or she should not be returned.

The need to escape

Refugees often have no choice but to enter another country without going through legal formalities. Article 31 of the UN Refugee Convention recognizes this reality. It says:

> "Contracting States shall not impose penalties, on account of their illegal entry or presence, on refugees who, coming directly from a territory where their life or freedom was threatened... enter or are present in their territory without authorization, provided they present themselves without delay to the authorities and show good cause for their illegal entry or presence."

This exemption from punishment for unauthorized entry applies to refugees whether or not they have yet been formally recognized; it therefore applies to asylum-seekers.

Refugees should not be punished for failing to possess valid travel documents or visas, or for using false documents. If the refugee could not have legally entered a country in order to escape persecution, this amounts to "good cause for their illegal entry".[14] To benefit from this provision, refugees have to present themselves to the authorities and ask for asylum "without delay", which should be taken to mean within a reasonable period of time. In some countries refugees are required to lodge their asylum claim within as little time as 24 hours. Such limits are clearly unreasonable given the circumstances of flight of many refugees.[15]

The term "coming directly" in Article 31 is often misused by states to deny protection to refugees. The drafters of the UN Refugee Convention intended to exclude those who "had settled temporarily" in one country before entering another, but not to

"We arrived here a year ago. The paramilitary were pressuring me to collaborate with them: 'Work with us or leave the area or die.' But to join up with them means working against our neighbours. That's why we had to leave."

A displaced *campesino* farmer now living in Barrancabermeja, Colombia, told his story to Amnesty International in June 1996. He continued:

"The paramilitary work together with the military. On 28 December 1994 I had to decide whether I was going to work with them or not. Then the army arrived while I was out working in the fields. They detained me and took me with them. I spent four days marching with them, tied up all the time. They beat me a lot and put a towel soaked in salty water over my face and a plastic bag over my head. All my body was black with bruises and even now you can see the scars. Finally the lieutenant ordered them to release me."

His wife added:

"The ordeal did not end there. They returned many times to the house, almost every day and night. They killed our neighbour and buried him... Our farm was left abandoned. Now we have no future. We cannot return. Our children are our future, but what future have we when we can't find work?"

Since 1985 over 750,000 people, mostly peasant families, have been internally displaced in Colombia by political violence which has left over 30,000 dead. Some were forced out because of military operations, others by threats or persecution from the Colombian armed forces, their paramilitary allies or armed opposition groups.

Forced to abandon their rural homes, deserting their livestock and possessions, they seek refuge in shanty towns surrounding towns and cities, where they, and particularly their children, may be preyed upon by urban "death squads". Fearing reprisals, most do not report the attacks and abuses which are the cause of their displacement and so their plight frequently goes unnoticed and they receive little or no assistance.

Children of a displaced family in San Pablo, Colombia
© Paul Smith/Panos Pictures

exclude refugees who had simply passed through other countries before arriving in the country where they sought asylum. The important issue is where the flight ends, not the countries that have been passed through during flight.

States are legitimately allowed to restrict the movements of refugees who have entered the country "illegally", but only on the basis that they "shall not apply to the movements of such refugees restrictions other than those which are necessary"[16] and only until their status is recognized or they obtain admission to another country.

Human rights in countries of asylum

Refugees' basic human rights in a country of asylum include liberty and security of the person, and protection from discrimination. Many other rights are spelled out in the UN Refugee Convention and other human rights treaties, such as the right to work, social security, public education and travel documents and the right to family reunion.[17] These depend on the refugee's status, whether they are lawfully in the territory and the host state's accession to refugee and other international treaties.

One of the most important human rights for refugees in their country of asylum is that of freedom from arbitrary arrest or detention. Human rights law has developed a series of measures to ensure that all individuals, including refugees, are not arbitrarily or unlawfully deprived of their liberty. The right to personal liberty is violated if an arrest or detention is arbitrary and is not carried out in accordance with a procedure prescribed by law. In many countries, asylum-seekers and refugees are automatically held in detention once they have asked for asylum. The UN Working Group on Arbitrary Detention, a body set up by the UN Commission on Human Rights, has declared:

> "[A]rticle 14 of the Universal Declaration of Human Rights guarantees the right to seek and to enjoy in other countries asylum from persecution. If detention in the asylum country results from exercising this right, such detention might be 'arbitrary'."

Freedom from arbitrary and unlawful detention includes the right to be brought promptly before a judicial authority; the right to review of detention within a reasonable time or to release; and the right to challenge detention before a competent authority.

Detailed rules governing the treatment of detainees and prisoners have been adopted by the UN. These are: the UN Standard
Minimum Rules for the Treatment of Prisoners; the UN Body of
Principles for the Protection of All Persons under Any Form of
Detention or Imprisonment; and the UN Rules for the Protection
of Juveniles Deprived of their Liberty. The Council of Europe
adopted similar rules in 1987 — the European Prison Rules.

There are a number of other international mechanisms that
can play a role in protecting detainees. These include: the Special
Rapporteur on torture; the Special Rapporteur on summary or
arbitrary executions; the UN Working Group on Enforced or
Involuntary Disappearances; the Committee against Torture; and
the Committee set up under the European Convention for the
Prevention of Torture and Inhuman or Degrading Treatment or
Punishment.

Human rights protection for particular groups

There are special additional human rights safeguards to protect
certain vulnerable groups, some of which are outlined below.

Women

Women are particularly vulnerable to discrimination and human
rights violations both before flight and as refugees. Despite this,
they can find it particularly difficult to claim refugee status success-
fully. For example, experience shows that women who suffer severe
discrimination on grounds of gender have difficulty proving that
the discrimination amounts to persecution. The UN Refugee Convention does not include gender as one of the specific grounds of
persecution on which to base a claim for refugee status. In addition,
asylum decision-makers often fail to understand the particular
difficulties and fears faced by women refugees.

The vast majority of women flee their country for the same
reasons as men — to escape persecution because of their national,
ethnic or social identity or their religious beliefs or political opin-
ions. Some forms of persecution, however, largely or exclusively
affect women. These should be accepted as valid grounds for granting protection under the UN Refugee Convention. Among the
issues that should be considered when assessing asylum claims by

women are the following:
- women may fear gender-related harm and may require gender-sensitive procedures during assessment of their claims;
- women may be persecuted for reasons of kinship, for example because of the activities of a male relative;
- women may be victims of severe discrimination on the basis of their gender, which may amount to persecution: often the state is unable or unwilling to protect them;
- women may be victims of acts of violence perpetrated by public authorities or private citizens (such as rape and domestic violence) which amount to persecution: again, often the state is unable or unwilling to protect them;
- women may be victims of human rights violations for transgressing or refusing to comply with their society's religious or customary laws and practices.

At present, official positions on which types of gender-related harm constitute persecution under the UN Refugee Convention vary between countries and are changing as individual cases are heard. One of the most progressive is the position adopted in 1993 and updated in 1996 by the Canadian Immigration and Refugee Board (IRB) in its guidelines for dealing with "Women Refugee Claimants Fearing Gender-Related Persecution". There has been much debate about the pros and cons of adding a new category of "gender" to the grounds for persecution in the UN Refugee Convention, or whether women making gender-related claims are covered in the category of "membership of a particular social group". The Canadian guidelines show how the existing refugee definition can be interpreted in a way that recognizes the relationship between gender and persecution, but stop short of adding gender as a ground for persecution. They have not yet been taken up by many other countries, although a few states, including Australia and the USA, have developed improved guidelines for considering women refugees fleeing gender-specific abuses, and others, among them Denmark and Switzerland, are in the process of drafting such guidelines.

Most gender-related claims made by women asylum-seekers raise four main issues, which the Canadian guidelines address:
- the extent to which a woman making a gender-related claim for asylum can rely on the reasons for persecution set out in

the UN Refugee Convention definition (race, religion, nationality, membership of a particular social group or political opinion);

● when sexual violence constitutes persecution;

● how decision-makers should gather and evaluate evidence;

● the special problems women face in describing the experiences that force them to seek asylum.

For women whose persecution is not based on grounds of race, religion, nationality or political opinion, the guidelines say that the category of "particular social group" should apply. The woman must be able to show that the "group" is distinguishable from the rest of the population. The "group" may hold some common belief or practice; it may suffer severe discrimination or inhuman treatment; it may be denied state protection from violence, including domestic violence. The fact that the "particular social group" may consist of large numbers of women is irrelevant: other Convention grounds, such as nationality and political opinion, are also characteristics shared by large numbers of people.

In 1991 UNHCR issued "Guidelines on the Protection of Refugee Women" and a number of Conclusions on women refugees have been issued by EXCOM. Among other things, the UNHCR Guidelines spell out the need for asylum procedures to take account of the special difficulties which refugee women may have when applying for asylum. For example, women may need to be given the opportunity to be interviewed alone by a woman official and with a woman interpreter.[18]

Whatever guidelines are adopted by individual governments, all states are obliged to protect women subject to their jurisdiction from human rights violations, including those suffered primarily or solely by women. The UN Declaration on the Elimination of Violence Against Women requires all states to work towards the eradication of violence against women. This means that women fleeing domestic violence committed in states which sanction or tolerate such abuses should be able to rely on the principles of the Declaration in demonstrating ways in which their state has failed to provide the protection to which they are entitled under international human rights standards.

Discrimination against women is prohibited in international human rights law. When discrimination amounts to persecution,

Neina* was blindfolded and lashed with an electric cable. Her interrogators continued whipping her as they screamed their questions. She can't remember how many times they hit her: the pain was too great. Finally she was released after signing a pledge that she would stop her political activities.

Unbowed, she continued handing out leaflets and selling newspapers for an Iranian opposition organization. The men in uniform came for her again. The torture was repeated. The whipping was repeated. And this time she was convicted and sentenced — to eight years in prison for entirely peaceful political activities.

She was released in 1991 but forced to report every month to Tehran's Evin Prison, the site of her worst nightmares. The last time she went, officials told her she would be imprisoned unless she recorded a video denouncing her political organization.

Neina was finally too scared to stay in the country she loved, even though, as she said, "I had considered escape... a form of treason". In the end, she fled to the Netherlands.

"In the Netherlands I was never treated as a political prisoner. Nobody took any notice of my psychological problems caused by the torture I endured. Without the assistance of Amnesty International, I probably would still be waiting for refugee status."

Today she is safe but not at peace. Her husband remains in Iran, undoubtedly in great danger, and one of her brothers is in prison. Although willing to have her case and this picture published, she is still nervous:

"Please don't write my name, my date of birth and my city, or any information that gives the regime a picture of me. After this time my name is Neina."

*pseudonym

such as when women are severely punished for breaking their society's customs, victims may qualify for protection under the UN Refugee Convention. The most important international treaty dealing with this issue is the Convention on the Elimination of All Forms of Discrimination against Women (CEDAW). This treaty obliges States Parties to condemn discrimination against women in all its forms, to adopt appropriate legislative and other measures, and to establish legal protection for the rights of women.

Further protection for women's rights is found in: the Convention on the Political Rights of Women; the Convention on the Nationality of Married Women; the Convention on Consent to Marriage, Minimum Age for Marriage and Registration of Marriages; and the UN Declaration on the Protection of Women and Children in Emergency and Armed Conflicts. In addition, the work of the Special Rapporteur on violence against women, appointed by the UN Commission on Human Rights in 1994, is instructive.

The Beijing Declaration and Platform for Action, adopted by the 1995 UN World Conference on Women, also contains important commitments by governments to improve the protection and promotion of women's human rights. For example, governments agreed to review national legislation, policies and practices in light of the CEDAW. Most importantly for refugee protection, governments recognized that sexual violence and other gender-related persecution constitute persecution within the meaning of the UN Refugee Convention. They also acknowledged that in some countries of asylum women have difficulties in being recognized as refugees when their claim is based on such persecution.

Children

Children are clearly a vulnerable group in need of special protection. The Convention on the Rights of the Child applies to all people under 18 years of age. It covers nearly every aspect of a child's life, from civil and political rights to health and education. There are specific provisions on juvenile justice, including deprivation of liberty, and on family rights. The Convention prohibits discrimination, which means that whatever benefits a state gives to children who are citizens, it must give to all children, including those who are refugees on its territory.[19]

Refugee children have special protection needs, especially

those who are alone (unaccompanied minors). UNHCR has published guidelines on appropriate procedures and EXCOM Conclusions 47 and 59 cover the special concerns of refugee children. Some states, notably Canada, have followed suit with similar guidelines.

The internally displaced

An estimated 25 to 30 million people have been uprooted from their homes and forced to flee in fear of their lives, but remain within the borders of their country of origin. As a result, they are deemed to be "internally displaced people", rather than refugees, by the international community. Most do not receive international protection and assistance.

Such people are particularly vulnerable to further abuses. Most are fleeing armed conflict and end up in camps, settlements or towns under the control of one of the parties to the conflict. As a result they often still face the same dangers they fled. Settlements in conflict zones are attacked, sometimes repeatedly. In camps, armed men enter to demand food, to abduct individuals, and to rape and abuse women and girls. In towns, internally displaced people often face extreme discrimination and abuse. In all these situations, they are economically marginalized, often destitute and have no outside authorities to turn to for help.

While the underlying causes for their flight may be identical to many of their compatriots who have fled abroad, only those who are outside their country have any chance of being recognized as refugees. This discrepancy has provoked widespread debate at an international level about the protection and assistance needs of the internally displaced. The debate has been fuelled by attempts by governments, the UN Security Council and UN agencies to deal with refugee flows by providing help to people in their own countries who might otherwise flee abroad.

The distinction between refugees and the internally displaced appears arbitrary, but doing away with it is not as simple as it might appear. Many governments are hostile to international involvement in protecting and assisting their own citizens, even if they are displaced, starving and sick. In some situations, the ferocity of the armed conflict makes it difficult to provide real protection. If "safe havens" are established, then governments in potential asylum countries will argue that displaced people should remain in the "safe haven" rather than seek protection abroad. Unfortunately, recent experiences in Bosnia and elsewhere show that "safe havens" are not necessarily safe at all.

In recent years the international community has paid more attention to internally displaced people. In 1991 the UN Commission on Human Rights adopted the first of several resolutions concerning the internally displaced. This led in 1992 to the appointment by the UN Secretary-General of a Representative for Internally Displaced Persons, who has studied relevant legal issues and held discussions with governments about how to improve the conditions of internally displaced people. In 1994 UNHCR issued guidelines on its own competence to work on behalf of the internally displaced. However, the steps taken so far by states and international organizations are inadequate. More needs to be done to protect the human rights of internally displaced people.

The key human rights of internally displaced people that need protection are the following:

- the right to freedom of movement within a state, including the freedom to choose one's own residence, and especially including the right not to be forcibly removed, relocated or otherwise forcibly displaced from one's chosen place of residence;
- absolute prohibitions on acts causing forcible displacement including:

   (i) forcible removals or relocations of members of national, ethnic, racial or religious groups which are carried out to create or maintain internal territorial divisions that are based on membership of such a group;

   (ii) forcible removals or relocations which cause serious physical or mental harm to members of a national, ethnic, racial or religious group or deliberately inflict on such a group conditions of life calculated to bring about its physical destruction, and which are committed with the intent to destroy, in whole or in part, such a group;

   (iii) deliberately provoking individuals to flee particular areas, through such measures as threats or use of violence or total disrespect for their fundamental human rights, or destruction of crops, livestock, water supplies, shelter or

"When I heard the shooting I picked up the baby and ran into the long grass. The shooting was in houses across our field. We lay hiding. It was becoming light. A soldier found us. He shot and killed the child. I was wounded but he went away."

Early that morning in May 1994 Aghok Lual Amuk, a young mother nursing her first child, had been asleep in her village two hours' walk from a strategically important railway line in Bahr al-Ghazal in Sudan.

Since 1983 her country had been racked by civil war. Aghok's village was in an area controlled by the rebel Sudan People's Liberation Army (SPLA). Each train bringing supplies to government-controlled garrisons in southern Sudan is escorted through the countryside by government troops and soldiers from the Popular Defence Force (PDF), a government militia.

The escorts destroy what they encounter — people, houses, crops and animals — to clear a path for the train and to destabilize areas under SPLA control by creating destitute displaced populations.

Aghok survived this particular attack. Other villagers were killed. The village was burned down and the entire cattle herd was looted. Aghok fled eastwards with scores of others — away from the railway to villages where food and medical care was available.

Since June 1994 these villages have been regularly assaulted by another government militia, often shortly after UN personnel have delivered relief supplies. Hundreds of people seeking food and security have been killed.

Aghok is among the millions of southern Sudanese and Nuba people displaced since the civil war in Sudan began. Bahr al-Ghazal is a remote part of a huge country — there is no nearby international border to offer sanctuary. Instead, people have to seek what safety they can in neighbours' land or in squatter camps that surround garrison towns and cities.

Around four million people are displaced in Sudan. © Sarah Errington/Panos Pictures

other materials essential to their survival, or in situations of conflict through acts intended to terrorize the civilian population or which are carried out with a deliberate disregard for their safety.

● the right of free movement should include the right of individuals within a state to flee (including to other countries if necessary) from areas where their lives, security or freedom are threatened, and the right not to be forcibly returned to such areas.

● the right of free movement should also include the right of internally displaced people to return to their homes should they wish to do so.

In addition, the internally displaced have rights to liberty and physical and mental integrity, to free opinion and expression and to freedom from arbitrary detention, unlawful killing or "disappearance" and torture or other cruel, inhuman or degrading treatment.

3 Circumvention of refugee law

Diabasana Natuba sought asylum in Germany after escaping from a Zairian military prison where she was tortured because she had been caught photocopying opposition party materials. The German authorities rejected her claim on several grounds. They stated that Zaire's President does not control the military and therefore torture by soldiers does not constitute state persecution. They asserted that she had committed a crime by photocopying documents, so her detention was legitimate. They said that the fact that she had travelled on a borrowed passport undermined her credibility. Most extraordinary of all, they said that her story was not credible because many other Zairians had recounted similar incidents. In mid-1996, she was sheltering in a church in Germany, terrified of being deported back to Zaire.

More and more refugees do not receive the international protection they need and deserve. Their rights as set down in international refugee and human rights law are routinely violated — by states that circumvent or have not ratified the refugee treaties, or by states that misinterpret or ignore the treaties they have ratified.

Avoidance of international obligations

By February 1997, 134 states had ratified either the UN Refugee Convention or the 1967 Protocol, and 126 had ratified both (see Appendix I). However, there are still more than 50 states which have ratified neither the Convention nor the Protocol.

In Asia, the majority of states have ratified neither the Convention nor the Protocol. In the Middle East (excluding north Africa), only three have ratified both the Convention and the Protocol — Iran, Israel and Yemen. The remaining 10 — Bahrain, Iraq, Jordan, Kuwait, Lebanon, Oman, Qatar, Saudi Arabia, Syria and the United Arab Emirates — have ratified neither.

In other regions the level of ratification is higher. In Africa, Comoros, Eritrea, Libya and Mauritius are the only countries that

The devastated city of Grozny, capital of the Chechen Republic.
© Martin Adler/ Panos Pictures

"They killed my 16-year-old daughter and three-month-old baby. How am I going to live now?"

Tears streamed down the face of 38-year-old Lidiya Morozovna Puchayeva as she told Amnesty International about the killing of two of her four children in March 1995 during a terrifying escape from the fighting in the Chechen Republic, part of the Russian Federation. Russian troops had fired on a convoy of vehicles carrying families trying to flee Achkhoy-Martan, which was being bombarded with shells. Seven of the refugees, including her two children, were shot dead.

Lidiya and other survivors ran for cover under a hail of bullets. Eventually they made their way to the Ingush Republic, also in Russia.

"My son and I were covered in blood...

We travelled in a convoy to Malgobek through military posts. Some people were good and took pity on us. Others we had to beg to let us through. We had to wait for hours, although I couldn't stand and I told them my son was injured too."

Lidiya Puchayeva is one of an estimated 300,000 Chechens who have been internally displaced in Russia as a result of the war in the Chechen Republic. Since Russian troops entered the republic in December 1994 to crush an independence movement, tens of thousands of civilians are said to have died in the fighting, many of them deliberately and unlawfully killed by soldiers. Others have been tortured and ill-treated in detention.

Lidiya cannot claim refugee status as she remains on Russian soil. She is just one of the millions of people worldwide who are "internally displaced".

have not ratified both treaties. In the Americas, Cuba, Guyana, Mexico and Trinidad and Tobago are not party to either of the treaties. In Europe only the relatively new states of Latvia, Moldova and Ukraine have not yet acceded to the Convention or the Protocol.

Surprisingly, five member states of EXCOM have signed neither the Convention nor the Protocol: Bangladesh, India, Lebanon, Pakistan and Thailand. All host substantial numbers of refugees and some of them flagrantly violate provisions of international refugee law. Yet their position on EXCOM gives them great influence over setting standards for international refugee protection.

Geographical limitation

The UN Refugee Convention gave states the option of protecting only refugees from Europe. To limit their obligations in this way, states had to make a declaration at the moment of accession. Such declarations were made by Monaco (1954), Turkey (1962), Congo (1962), Madagascar (1967), Malta (1971) and Hungary (1989).[20]

The 1967 Protocol removed the geographical limitation. The only exception was that states that had already declared geographical limitations before 1967 were permitted to retain them. This was taken up by Congo, Monaco and Turkey.[21] However, Malta and Hungary, both of which acceded to the Convention and the Protocol after 1967, still made a geographical limitation even though they were not formally entitled to do so.[22]

Governments that have not ratified the international refugee treaties have contended that if they did so they would be forced to accept large numbers of refugees. The same argument has been used by states that refuse to rescind geographical limitations. Turkey, for example, refuses to undertake obligations towards refugees from neighbouring non-European countries. Turkish officials often complain that the pressure from Western European governments to remove the limitation is unfair since Western European countries are less accessible to potential refugee flows from the Middle East and Asia than Turkey. It is unlikely that states will be persuaded to extend their obligations until the wealthier countries share more fully the global responsibility for hosting refugees.

Esther Kiobel and Blessing Kpuinen became asylum-seekers after both their husbands were hanged by the Nigerian authorities. On 10 November 1995, nine Ogoni prisoners, mostly members of the Movement for the Survival of the Ogoni People (MOSOP), were executed after grossly unfair and politically motivated trials. The best-known outside Nigeria was the writer Ken Saro-Wiwa. Two of the others were Dr Barinem Kiobel and John Kpuinen.

Ogoni activists have been systematically targeted by the Nigerian authorities because of MOSOP's campaign against environmental damage by multinational oil companies — notably Shell — and its demands for increased autonomy for the Ogoni ethnic group. MOSOP members have been harassed, detained, tortured and killed by the security forces.

The Ogoni trials were a travesty of justice. The victims were seized during a wave of arrests of MOSOP supporters after the murder of four Ogoni leaders in May 1994. They were detained incommunicado and without charge for months in harsh and insanitary conditions. Some said in court

Blessing Kpuinen

that they had been tortured. The special tribunal appointed to try them was neither independent nor impartial. It decided that any senior member of MOSOP deemed to have contributed to a civil disturbance could be convicted of murder. It reversed the burden of proof, so that defendants without alibis were found to have been present at the murders. It allowed no right of appeal.

Every day Esther and Blessing would take food for their husbands in prison, even though this meant they suffered harassment, assaults and even detention in harsh conditions. On 10 November they were turned away and threatened with guns. They eventually went home. Hours later they learned that their husbands had been hanged and buried earlier that day.

Shortly afterwards, the two women sought asylum in neighbouring Benin to escape the continuing arrests and persecution of the families and supporters of the executed Ogoni activists.

Esther Kiobel

Restrictive interpretations of the refugee definition

The proportion of asylum-seekers recognized as refugees varies enormously, from around 70 per cent in Canada to between one and 20 per cent in Scandinavia and other European countries. Since there is no international judicial body to rule on questions of interpretation, the result is that there may be wide differences in how the UN Refugee Convention definition is interpreted between one country and another. The following are just a few illustrative examples of overly restrictive or insupportable interpretations used by governments to reject refugees.

● **Torture and ill-treatment considered an individual act**

Asylum authorities often treat torture and ill-treatment as illegal acts of violence by individual officials, rather than state persecution. Tortured refugees are refused recognition even when there is clear evidence of endemic torture and ill-treatment in the country they have fled.

● **Fear of future persecution is not enough**

Some states argue that someone who was not persecuted in the past cannot have a well-founded fear of persecution in the future. Evidence of past persecution is a strong indication of future risk. Fear of future persecution is a central part of the definition of a refugee, and establishing this is not dependent on having already suffered persecution. The assessment of a refugee claim is essentially an estimate of what may happen in the future.

● **Political persecution treated as punishment for a criminal act**

Political persecution because of membership of a banned but non-violent organization or participation in a peaceful demonstration is treated by some asylum authorities as part of the normal process of law. This interpretation has been applied even to refugees coming from countries that systematically violate human rights, such as Iraq.

● **Punishment for desertion treated as legitimate**

Punishment for desertion or for refusal to serve in the military, even if the punishment is death, is often not accepted as grounds for granting asylum. This is applied even to people fleeing wars such as those in former Yugoslavia and in the Gulf.

● **Human rights violations in civil wars not treated as persecution**

Persecution which takes place in the framework of counter-insurgency operations or civil wars is frequently not considered

Haitian asylum-seekers being repatriated from Guantánamo Bay, a US naval base, in 1994

Following orders is no defence for carrying out human rights violations. Yet disobeying orders to commit inhumane acts and taking a stand against state-sanctioned murder was no guarantee that Vilvert Exumé, a Haitian soldier, would receive the protection of the US authorities.

On 28 November 1987 — the night before the long-awaited elections in Haiti — Vilvert Exumé was stationed at the Fort Dimanche military camp outside the capital, Port-au-Prince. An army truck arrived carrying more than a dozen young men. The prisoners were dragged from the truck, shoved against a wall and shot in the head. Vilvert Exumé was ordered to guard the bodies while soldiers went to get another truck-load of prisoners. Miraculously, one prisoner was still alive. He pleaded with Vilvert to help him. Vilvert cut the rope binding his hands and pointed to a path in the jungle.

Vilvert was interrogated about the missing body. He was jailed for five months and subjected to mock executions and

beatings to make him confess. Finally, on 1 May 1988, he was dishonourably discharged. Soon after, the escaped prisoner gave a radio interview describing his ordeal and Vilvert Exumé knew that his life was at risk. He hid for 10 months before escaping to Miami, USA.

His treatment by the US authorities highlights the problems faced by many Haitian asylum-seekers at that time. He was detained for more than 14 months, mostly in a camp in Laredo, Texas, where his access to legal services was extremely limited. In July 1990 his application for asylum was rejected on the grounds that he had been forced to flee not because of his beliefs, but because he had disobeyed orders and his fear was therefore of "prosecution not persecution". The judgment took no account of the widespread human rights violations in Haiti at the time.

Vilvert Exumé appealed and his application for asylum was finally accepted in May 1993, more than four years after he arrived in the USA.

grounds for asylum, even if the asylum-seekers or their relatives have suffered gross human rights abuses. It is true that the requirement of a "well-founded fear of persecution" implies that a refugee must be individually at risk of persecution. But it is also clear that the refugee definition applies in situations where an entire group has been displaced and members of the group are at risk of human rights violations because of some shared, albeit individual, characteristic.

● Persecution other than by the state

In France and Germany the UN Refugee Convention criteria for who is deserving of protection is not extended to include persecution by people other than state agents, such as armed opposition groups and private individuals, known as "non-state actors". They also deny recognition as a refugee to those at risk of persecution when the authority of the state has broken down. This goes against the stated intention of the UN Refugee Convention that protection should be given to those whom the state is unwilling or unable to protect, and goes against the spirit of protecting those at risk of persecution.

4 Obstructing and deterring asylum-seekers

Barriers to access

During the past few years many states have taken measures to obstruct refugees trying to reach their countries and their asylum procedures. New visa requirements, fines on airlines and shipping companies for transporting people without travel documents or visas, interdiction on the high seas and pre-flight screening of passengers are major examples of such restrictive measures.

Nearly all Western European countries imposed a visa requirement on people from Bosnia-Herzegovina after mid-1992, when the war had started and a large number of people were trying to escape generalized violence as well as torture, rape and political killings. They then offered the refugees "temporary protection" (see Chapter 6).

The same raising of barriers against fleeing refugees was seen after the military coup in Haiti in September 1991, when supporters of the deposed President were arbitrarily arrested, tortured and killed. Approximately 300 Haitian refugees arrived in France and Switzerland in the months after the coup. Switzerland did not require visas at that time; France had required Haitians to have an entry visa for several years. Despite the relatively small number involved, during 1992 Switzerland imposed a visa requirement on Haitians and France imposed a transit visa requirement on Haitians travelling to other destinations.

Most Haitian refugees tried to reach the USA in the months after the coup and more than 38,000 risked their lives at sea. In June 1992 the USA intercepted Haitian boat people at sea and summarily returned them, without any examination of their asylum claims. This directly violated the principle of *non-refoulement*. Other Haitian refugees intercepted at sea languished in the US base at Guantánamo Bay awaiting screening by US and UNHCR officials.

An Iraqi Kurdish father (left) buries his child on the border between Iraq and Iran. The child had died during the family's flight from Iraq.
© David Stewart-Smith

The US Supreme Court ruled that the interception of Haitians in coastal waters by US naval officials did not violate the principle of *non-refoulement*.[23] The ruling was a perverse reading of this customary norm of international law and is widely regarded as representing a political rather than judicially sound interpretation of international refugee law.

Many states fine airlines and shipping companies if they carry people who do not have travel documents. As a result, some airlines conduct pre-flight screenings at points of embarkation, especially at airports where potential asylum-seekers are expected to leave. Immigration officials from some industrialized countries have been dispatched to refugee-producing countries to train airline check-in staff to spot passengers with suspect papers or motives and to prevent them boarding. Several members of the European Union (EU) have adopted such practices, despite a resolution passed by the European Parliament that all asylum-seekers should have automatic and unfettered access to admission procedures, and that visa policies and sanctions on carriers should not be an impediment to such access.[24]

Many governments ignore their international obligation not to punish refugees who have entered the country "illegally".[25] In Europe some countries, such as Austria, the Baltic states, Bulgaria, Poland and Russia, refuse to make any exemptions in their laws for asylum-seekers who enter the country "illegally". Others, including Albania, France, Germany, Romania, the Slovak Republic and Turkey, do not generally penalize asylum-seekers for "illegal" entry, although they may be detained and require legal intervention to ensure release. Those that do have laws exempting asylum-seekers who enter the country "illegally" include Azerbaijan, Belgium, Greece, Hungary, Italy, Portugal, Spain and Sweden.[26] However, even in these countries such laws are not always applied consistently, notably in Belgium.

Measures that obstruct the entry of asylum-seekers, including visa requirements and carrier sanctions, are incompatible with the intention of Articles 31 and 33 of the UN Refugee Convention. This view is also supported by various EXCOM conclusions.

Rejection at the border

Border officials should never be allowed to decide an asylum

Thirsty and exhausted asylum-seekers from Liberia aboard leaky boats were turned away from one port after another. In the West African heat, thousands of men, women and children had crammed into rusting freighters with little food or water, practically no sanitation, and no certainty of when or where they would be allowed to land. They knew conditions would be dire. There was not even enough room to lie down and sleep. Yet their fear of the bloodshed at home drove them to risk their lives at sea in a desperate bid to escape.

The plight of these refugees starkly reveals how harsh the world has become for asylum-seekers, even in Africa with its long tradition of hospitality and its wider definition of who is a refugee. After more than six years of civil war, about three quarters of a million Liberians have been driven from their homes and have found asylum in other West African countries, with more than 400,000 in Guinea, over 300,000 in Côte d'Ivoire, and thousands more in Sierra Leone, Ghana and Nigeria.

In April 1996, after several months of relative calm in Liberia, bitter fighting broke out again in the capital, Monrovia, between rival armed groups. The civilian population was terrorized as mortars and gunfire filled the air. Armed faction members roamed the streets, looting, maiming and killing.

Thousands of frantic people took refuge in the compounds of foreign embassies in Monrovia. Thousands more bought tickets for ships that would take them away from the carnage. Over the next two months, some half dozen boats carried refugees away from Liberia.

But escaping from Monrovia proved easier than gaining access to safe asylum. Numerous West African states, including Côte d'Ivoire, Ghana and Sierra Leone, refused to allow passengers to land and seek asylum. Government officials prevented refugees leaving the boats, despite the appalling conditions, the desperation of the refugees, and the pleas of UN and agency officials. Several people died on board the ships before the human cargoes were eventually allowed to disembark.

© Jon Spaull

application; they should be explicitly instructed to refer all such cases to the responsible authority. EXCOM has stated that there must be a clearly identified authority responsible for examining requests for refugee status and that a frontier authority should not reject an asylum claim without reference to that authority.[27] In practice, however, border officials often refuse to allow refugees without proper documents to enter the country to seek asylum. Border officials should be instructed and trained in their duty to respect the principle of *non-refoulement*.[28]

When refugees are rejected at the border they will be sent back to their persecutors, sent to another country where they could be at risk of human rights violations or *refoulement*, or forced to enter the country of asylum illegally and possibly face punishment for "illegal entry".

Detention

Fatema fled to Sweden for safety. She had been raped and badly beaten by political opponents in Bangladesh in two separate incidents, sustaining head injuries and permanent damage to an eye. Instead of giving her the protection she sought, the Swedish authorities put her into detention. They refused her lawyer's request for a full medical examination and finally deported her to Bangladesh. All over the world, far too many people like Fatema are detained, sometimes for long periods, simply because they sought asylum from persecution.

In Africa, for example, refugee status and the benefits that go with it often depend on the refugee remaining in designated camps or zones. This is sometimes for the refugees' protection, or to facilitate assistance programs, but sometimes it can act as a form of detention — no one should have to choose between food and freedom of movement.

In Europe and North America detention of asylum-seekers has increased dramatically as states make strenuous efforts to deter and obstruct refugees from seeking asylum in their countries. In Australia asylum-seekers who arrive without prior authorization are automatically detained. In some countries, asylum-seekers are detained as soon as they arrive and are held while their application is processed. In others, specific groups of asylum-seekers are placed behind bars, for example those whose applications are considered "manifestly unfounded" (see Chapter 5). Other countries regularly detain rejected asylum-seekers pending deportation.

There are very few accurate statistics on the number of refugees detained, the length of their imprisonment or where they come from. Official figures fail to distinguish between asylum-seekers and aliens who are being held for other reasons. Also, the definition of "detention" varies. In some countries asylum-seekers held at the airport or confined in a reception centre or camp are not registered as being in detention. Amnesty International believes that if someone is deprived of their liberty, whether in a prison, a detention centre, a closed camp or any other restricted area, that person must be considered to be in detention.

EXCOM has stated that the detention of asylum-seekers "should normally be avoided"[29]. Detention is allowed by international standards only:

- if it is necessary, and
- if it is lawful and not arbitrary, and
- if it is for one of the following reasons:

(i) "to verify identity";

(ii) "to determine the elements on which the claim to refugee status or asylum is based";

(iii) "to deal with cases where refugees or asylum-seekers have destroyed their travel or identity documents or have used fraudulent documents in order to mislead the authorities of the State in which they intend to claim asylum";

(iv) "to protect national security or public order".[30]

These conditions place the onus on the detaining authorities to demonstrate why other measures short of detention are not sufficient. Moreover, even if an asylum-seeker is detained legitimately, detention should not continue for longer than is necessary. For example, detention "to verify identity" or "to determine the elements on which the claim to refugee status or asylum is based" should be permitted only until a preliminary interview can be carried out.[31] In most cases, this should not require more than one or two days.

In practice, states ignore or misinterpret these requirements. For example, asylum-seekers who have had to use false documentation to escape their country are detained on the grounds that they were trying to mislead the asylum authorities about their identity.[32]

"The police sprayed gas into the room and shut the door... When the policeman ordered me to leave the room he hit me again with his stick, this time on the shoulder. I tried to stand up, but I slipped and fell to the ground. The officer then kicked me in the lower back."

This is not a refugee's account of persecution in her country of origin. It is her account of how she was treated after she asked for asylum in the USA.

Fauziya Kasinga sought sanctuary to escape female genital mutilation. In her home country of Togo, her wealthy father had protected her from the practice which causes lifelong injury to millions of women worldwide. However, after his sudden death, her aunt removed her from school and married her off to a man three times her age, who insisted she undergo genital mutilation. Just days before it was to be carried out, her sister helped her to escape.

When she arrived in the USA she immediately asked for asylum. She felt sure that she would find sanctuary in a country that "believed in justice". To her shock, she was transported to Esmor detention centre in handcuffs and shackles. Just 17 years old, for the first time in her life she was forced to strip naked in front of a stranger. Conditions in Esmor were harsh: poor food, filthy clothing, lack of heat, insect-infested bedding and theft of detainees' belongings by staff. After disturbances in June 1995 were violently quelled by guards using sticks and tear-gas, an official report concluded that guards had treated inmates with capricious cruelty.

Fauziya was held in various prisons for more than a year. In August 1995 an immigration judge rejected her asylum claim, saying "this alien is not credible". Despite repeated requests, she was refused release pending the outcome of her appeal until April 1996. She was finally granted asylum in a landmark decision recognizing that female genital mutilation can be a form of persecution that entitles its victims to international protection.

To ensure that detention lasts only as long as necessary, the reasons for detention and its necessity should be automatically reviewed at regular intervals by a judicial or similar authority.

The decision to detain asylum-seekers is sometimes arbitrary. It may rest on factors such as the availability of detention places and the attitude of the official involved, rather than on an objective assessment of whether detention is actually necessary and justified. Too often, decisions to detain reflect social stereotypes and biases.

Asylum-seekers and refugees are often not only deprived of their liberty, but also held in conditions that amount to cruel, inhuman or degrading treatment. Some commit suicide in despair; others die of illnesses or medical neglect in detention. Michael Akhimen, an asylum-seeker from Nigeria, was detained in Canada in October 1995. At the end of November he stated: "I can no longer stay in detention when I have committed no crime and my family back home cannot be located." On 18 December 1995 Michael Akhimen died; he had reportedly not received adequate medical attention. Amnesty International was not satisfied that the investigation into his death in custody was adequate.

Sometimes the physical conditions of detention for asylum-seekers are worse than those for convicted criminals serving sentences in prison, yet those seeking asylum have not been convicted of any crime. Asylum-seekers are frequently detained in shoddy temporary shelters or in centres run by private companies that are less well regulated by the authorities than prisons. In the USA, asylum-seekers are frequently moved from one detention centre to another, sometimes far from their families or legal representatives. Australia's main detention facility for asylum-seekers in Port Hedland is thousands of miles away from any major city and access to legal counsel is a major problem. In addition, detained refugees suffer the psychological torment of not knowing for how long they will be held and are in constant fear that they may be sent back to their persecutors. Torture victims in particular suffer further trauma through the psychological stress of detention.

As well as the right not to be arbitrarily detained, under international standards asylum-seekers and refugees have the following rights if they are in detention:

- right of access to legal counsel;[33]
- right to communicate with UNHCR;[34]

Two Zairian women, both traumatized after being raped by state officials, travelled to the United Kingdom (UK) at different times hoping to find security. Their hopes were short-lived.

The first, Marie,* was found wandering around London airport in 1993, alone and confused. A few days earlier she had been gang-raped by five or six soldiers in her home in Kinshasa, capital of Zaire. Her husband, a member of an opposition group, had "disappeared".

Marie's application for asylum in the UK was refused. On appeal, the adjudicator dismissed her appeal but recommended that, given her suffering, she be allowed to stay on compassionate grounds. This was ignored. In March 1995 the government made arrangements to deport her to Zaire. She went into hiding and at the end of the year was granted one year's leave to remain.

At least she received welfare payments to buy food and shelter. Another Zairian woman, Bénédicte,* was denied this basic right. She arrived in the UK in February 1996, days after a legal ruling that only those who apply for asylum immediately at the port of entry are eligible to receive welfare payments while the claim is assessed. The process can take more than 19 months.

Bénédicte had been arrested in Zaire at a memorial for her husband, who had been shot dead during an anti-government rally. In prison she was repeatedly raped by guards. An older guard finally took pity on her and smuggled her out in a sack.

She arrived in London by train, and then made her way to the Home Office, some miles away, where she applied for asylum. She was subsequently denied welfare payments on the grounds that she had not applied for asylum immediately on arrival.

A legal challenge was made to the Court of Appeal about the denial of welfare payments, which ruled in her favour. One of the judges stated:

"A significant number of genuine asylum-seekers now find themselves faced with a bleak choice: whether to remain here destitute and homeless until their claims are finally determined or whether instead to abandon their claims and return to face the very persecution they have fled."

The legal victory was short-lived. In July 1996, the British parliament passed legislation denying welfare payments to all those who failed to apply for asylum immediately on arrival and to people appealing against rejection of their asylum claim. However, in October a new High Court ruling required local government authorities to provide some assistance to asylum-seekers. In December, for the first time in 50 years, the Red Cross distributed food parcels in London, the capital. The recipients were destitute asylum-seekers.

*pseudonym

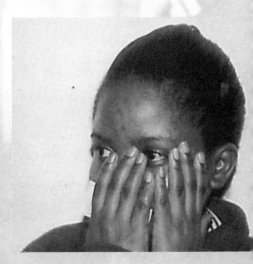

Marie

- right to notify their family of the fact and place of detention;[35]
- right to be visited by, and to correspond with, members of their family;[36]
- right to communicate with the outside world;[37]
- right to medical care;[38]
- right to humane conditions of detention, which take into account their special status as asylum-seekers; they should not be held in places where their physical safety is endangered and they should not be held with common criminals;[39]
- refugee children should not be detained.[40]

Destitution

In the UK, new legislation has denied many asylum-seekers access to social benefits, leaving them destitute and dependent on charity. In other countries, particularly in the developing world, large numbers of refugees are given no means of sustenance. Such circumstances have forced refugees to return home to danger and have resulted in serious damage to their health. The lack of subsistence provision for refugees also deters other refugees who would otherwise seek refuge in those countries.

The withdrawal of basic subsistence is not in keeping with the humanitarian spirit of the UN Refugee Convention and in some cases might amount to *refoulement*. If asylum-seekers are induced to abandon their claims because they cannot survive, states are undermining their obligation to provide fair and effective access to asylum procedures.

5 Asylum procedures

All states that are party to the UN Refugee Convention are obliged to consider claims for asylum. A fair and satisfactory asylum determination procedure provides the strongest guarantees for identifying properly those at risk and ensuring that the principle of *non-refoulement* is respected.

A large number of refugees around the world are given protection in other countries on a group basis because they have fled en masse from catastrophic human rights situations. People fleeing civil wars, widespread violence and massive human rights violations are allowed to remain in host countries, often on the basis of their nationality or ethnic group.

Some countries have established no procedures for granting asylum to individuals. Some have procedures that are grossly inadequate. Some have adopted a dual approach, allowing groups of refugees to remain, as well as having procedures for individual claims. This chapter looks in general terms at the issues relating to situations of mass exodus and in some detail at individual asylum procedures that largely apply in industrialized countries.

Mass exodus

Mass exoduses are caused by mass human rights violations. This is the reality that defines the need for protection and assistance of those who are forced to flee as part of a mass movement, as well as their prospects for returning home. When hundreds of thousands of people flee their country, other states are obliged to admit them at least on a temporary basis. This has implications for the country in which refugees first seek refuge and for the international community, which must help find durable solutions. To date, governments' responses to situations of mass exodus have varied and have been influenced by the size and nature of the refugee population, the political and economic circumstances of the host state, and the support — or lack of it — received from the international community.

However difficult the circumstances, all governments must

The ruined town of Turanj, in eastern Croatia, where thousands of Bosnian refugees sought shelter.
© Sebastião Salgado

Assam is a nurse who was politically active in Iran. She worked as a volunteer with people injured in the Iran-Iraq war and belonged to the leftist Tudeh party.

"The situation in Iran at that time was very difficult for active people. There were very many arrests and they did not distinguish between different levels of activity, so that one could be arrested just because of having sold a book. The situation was particularly critical for women. This was because they were not considered to have 'much of a brain' and it was therefore inappropriate to undertake political activity.

"I was told by the Iranian authorities to come for interrogation and then I realized that my life was in danger." Political detainees in Iran are routinely tortured, and many have been executed after summary trials.

She travelled to Sweden via Turkey, but on arrival was told she should have applied for asylum in Turkey and was sent back there. Turkey does not recognize as refugees individuals from two of the largest groups of asylum-seekers in the country, Iraqis and Iranians. Many have been sent back to their countries of origin to face torture and other serious human rights violations.

Assam managed to get back to Sweden, where her asylum application was rejected several times. She was about to be deported when a letter arrived from a court prosecutor in Iran saying that she had been charged and would be tried. She was then granted asylum.

"It was horrible having to wait so long for a decision. When I think back it was like torture, every day seemed to be as long as a year. It is no fun to come to a country knowing nobody. I was only 21 years old and I did it only to save my life. The day I learn that I can go back to Iran safely, I shall return."

respect the fundamental principle of *non-refoulement*. This means that asylum-seekers should not be rejected at the frontier and should not be forcibly removed to a place where they may be at risk of persecution or grave human rights violations. The obligations this places on countries of first asylum are only sustainable if the international community helps to find durable solutions for the refugees, whether this means resettlement elsewhere, repatriation when safe, or integration into the host state. If the international community fails to find solutions, then states hosting large numbers of refugees are put in a very difficult position. While it is never acceptable for states to forcibly return people to a situation of risk, it is also unacceptable for the international community to fail to live up to its responsibility to ensure that long-term solutions are found.

In situations of mass exodus it is not possible, and not usually necessary, to provide for an individual determination of the need for protection of refugees on their arrival. There is, in effect, a *prima facie* presumption of refugee status based on the nature of the movement and the causes of flight. This initial form of protection may be provided by temporary protection schemes, such as that applied recently in Western Europe, or according to the more advanced standards provided by the OAU Refugee Convention. Whatever practices apply, it is crucial that all refugees are allowed to cross borders and that no one is subject to *refoulement*. It is also important that all refugees are afforded the rights that would normally apply under the UN Refugee Convention.

When it is deemed that refugees in situations of mass exodus can return home in safety, there should always be an opportunity for those who do not wish to return to identify themselves as having individual grounds for continuing to fear persecution if returned. Their cases should then be considered individually in a fair and satisfactory asylum procedure.

Individual asylum procedures

The process followed in deciding asylum claims is of vital importance. There are lives at stake. Yet every day asylum-seekers face problems when asking for sanctuary. Sometimes the person deciding the asylum claim does not personally interview the claimant or does not have sufficient impartial information about conditions in the asylum-seeker's country of origin. Sometimes the asylum-seeker is too frightened to explain fully to an official their reasons for flight or is not asked to give details of the persecution they fear, and later this is used as an argument to refuse asylum. In some cases, there is no interpreter available or the interpreter translates inaccurately. In some countries when an application is rejected, written reasons for the decision are not given. These are just a few of the main concerns that Amnesty International has about the inadequacies of asylum determination procedures.

Fair and satisfactory asylum procedures

Amnesty International believes that the minimum requirements for a fair and satisfactory asylum procedure as outlined below should be universally applied. An asylum hearing is only fair and satisfactory when the following requirements are fulfilled:

● **Independent and specialized decision-making body.**

The body responsible for deciding asylum claims must be independent and specialized, with sole and exclusive responsibility for dealing with such claims. Its composition must ensure decision-making that is independent, based on human rights and refugee law, and not influenced by other considerations such as national immigration and foreign policy. The assessment of an asylum claim can involve complex questions of refugee law and human rights law, and often requires detailed information about the situation in the claimant's country of origin. Officials should be provided with objective and independent information on the human rights situation in countries of origin or any countries to which asylum-seekers might be sent. Decision-makers should not rely on information about the claimant's country of origin or case that is not disclosed to the claimant, such as secret reports.

● **Qualified decision-maker.**

Every asylum claim, whether submitted on arrival or after entry into the country, should be examined in the first instance by an official of the responsible decision-making body, who should interview the applicant personally. This official should have expertise in international human rights law and refugee law, and should also have knowledge of the human rights situation in the asylum-seeker's country of origin. The status and tenure of the decision-makers should afford the strongest possible guarantees of their competence, impartiality and independence.

Fawaz Housein El-Hanafy is a Palestinian. Like so many other Palestinians, he has never been allowed to visit the land of his ancestors. His parents fled Palestine in 1948, eventually settling as refugees in Kuwait where Fawaz was born in 1966.

After the Gulf War, armed civilians and military personnel roamed the streets in Kuwait hunting down non-Kuwaitis, including Palestinians, especially young men suspected of collaboration with Iraqi forces. Twice they came to the family home to arrest Fawaz, but twice he managed to escape. Shortly after, his family was forcibly expelled from Kuwait. Fawaz explains:

"I had not committed any crime and had not cooperated with the Iraqi army. However, I felt a threat... because persecution against Palestinians was done indiscriminately...

"It is so sad to leave family. But... I said to myself that I could meet my family somewhere sometime if I could stay alive."

Fawaz fled to India on a student visa, knowing that he would be permanently denied re-entry to the country of his birth. When his student visa was about to expire, he obtained a visa for Japan. He flew there in November 1991 and applied for asylum.

Although confused by the complicated and secretive asylum procedures in Japan, and upset that he was provided with a translator who could not speak Arabic, he was confident that the wide publicity given to the persecution of Palestinians in Kuwait would guarantee his asylum. A year later, however, his application was rejected.

Lawyers and the Amnesty International Japanese section took up his case and in December 1995 he was finally granted refugee status. His was the first appeal case in 15 years to succeed among more than 300 other filed appeals.

"Dreams start to come true," he says. "I got married to a Japanese woman... I will have the chance to go and visit my family after six years... I start to feel that I belong to this society and the society belongs to me."

The decision-maker should take into account that asylum-seekers who have been persecuted by the authorities in their own country may feel apprehensive towards all officials and may be afraid to speak freely about their case. The decision-maker should gain the confidence of the asylum-seeker to help the applicant explain the grounds for seeking asylum. So, for example, women asylum-seekers should be offered the opportunity of being heard by a woman. A woman who was raped by a soldier should not be expected to talk about her experiences to another man.

All officials involved in questioning or interviewing asylum-seekers and in making decisions on their applications should be instructed and trained to follow the procedural guidance given in UNHCR's Handbook on Procedures and Criteria for Determining Refugee Status.

● **Qualified interpreter**

Competent, qualified and impartial interpreters should be available throughout all stages of the asylum process. The asylum-seeker must be able to trust the interpreter and the interpreter should faithfully state what the claimant says, rather than generalize or summarize.

● **Individual and thorough examination**

Every asylum claim should be dealt with individually by a thorough examination of the circumstances of the case. The complexity of the refugee definition and the need to make judgments about future risks make every case different.

● **Legal assistance**

Asylum-seekers are vulnerable and cannot be expected to know how to exercise their rights in the asylum procedure. It is essential that asylum-seekers are able to obtain effective legal assistance and are advised of this right. They should be granted access to UNHCR at all stages of the process and to appropriate non-governmental organizations.

● **Reasonable time**

Asylum-seekers should be given a reasonable time to prepare their case and to seek legal and other advice. There is a tendency in many European and North American countries to speed up the procedures, sometimes allowing only two or three days to prepare a case or to launch an appeal. At the same time there is also a tendency to require asylum-seekers to provide more and more proof of persecution, such as arrest warrants, military call-up orders or medical reports.

● **Benefit of the doubt**

Most people who have fled from their home country arrive with the barest necessities and frequently without personal documents. It is not always possible for asylum-seekers to "prove" every part of their case and it is often necessary to give the applicant the benefit of the doubt.[41]

Right to appeal

The right to appeal is essential. The appeal process should include the following:

● **Reasons for rejection explained**

Any rejection of an asylum request should be given to the asylum-seeker in writing. It should clearly state the reasons for the rejection, including an assessment of the evidence, the documentary evidence relied upon and the relevant laws and facts. The asylum-seeker should also receive clear instructions on how to appeal. Asylum-seekers can only appeal effectively against an incorrect decision if they know what considerations have led to the decision.

● **Independent appeal body**

An appeal against an initial decision to deny asylum should be to a different body. It should be a judicial authority, such as a court, or at least a higher administrative authority. Given the evidence of inconsistent decision-making in similar cases at the first instance, it is important that the appeal body examines the merits of the individual case and all relevant facts.

● **Right to stay during the appeal procedure**

The asylum-seeker should be allowed to remain in the country where they have sought asylum until the outcome of the appeal has been finally decided. To deport an asylum-seeker to the country of origin before a final decision on appeal renders the right of appeal meaningless. This "suspensive effect" on expulsions should be applied in all cases.

Shortcomings in asylum procedures

The major shortcomings in asylum procedures include the following:

● **"Manifestly unfounded" claims**

Ebenezer Koomson was widely praised in the German news media for his bravery during the fire that destroyed much of Dusseldorf airport in April 1996. Journalists paid tribute to his courage in helping people escape and in guiding the fire brigade despite the smoke and heat.

He was not always made so welcome. He describes his first interview for asylum:

"The interviewing officer suddenly shouted at me to remove my hands from my pockets when I am talking to him — and I immediately responded. There was this dreadful feeling of hell and nobodyness. I remember clutching my children close to me. I looked all around me, begging soundlessly with my eyes for help, only to see blank faces."

Ebenezer Koomson fled from Ghana in January 1982, believing that his life was in danger. He first went to Togo, but when he felt that his life was once again threatened, he fled to Germany in June 1983 with his two-year-old daughter and his son. After two long years of asylum appeals, uncertainty and anxiety, he was finally given refugee status.

"The relief when one finally finds a safe place where suddenly all your worries vanish — it's like heaven. You can't describe it. It's like a miracle. It's like having a second chance in life."

Ebenezer has grabbed his second chance eagerly and has more than repaid Germany's hospitality. He is now the personnel manager for all the restaurants in Dusseldorf airport and is responsible for about 400 staff. Sixteen people died in the airport fire, but even more would have been killed without his selfless intervention.

Special circumstances may warrant the exceptional treatment of an asylum claim or a group of claims from people in a similar situation. These circumstances may include, for example, a determination that an asylum claim is "manifestly unfounded" in the sense that it is clearly fraudulent or not related to the criteria for granting refugee status laid down in the UN Refugee Convention. Such exceptional treatment should only permit an appeal to be expedited. Asylum-seekers must still be allowed to remain until the appeal has been decided.

There is an increasing tendency for asylum requests to be screened out as "manifestly unfounded" on the basis that they are without merit or because asylum could have been sought elsewhere. Some European governments have drawn up "white lists" of countries, which presume that no one fleeing any of the named countries would be in danger if returned home. In some host countries the failure to hold valid travel documents or the use of false documents render an asylum application "manifestly unfounded" or subject to "fast-track" or "accelerated airport procedures" (see below). These grounds for rejecting claims fail to recognize the individual character of flight. It is not possible to decide whether an individual has a well-founded fear of persecution without examining their case, regardless of which country they come from.

In most countries applications from refugees that are designated "manifestly unfounded" or "inadmissible" have been dealt with in summary procedures. The applications have not been individually and thoroughly examined, and the people concerned have no right to appeal, or only a very limited right to appeal. Such practices are unfair and unsatisfactory.

● **"Accelerated airport procedures"**

"Accelerated airport procedures" applied to asylum-seekers arriving from "safe" countries of origin or without valid documents enable host states to decide on the person's asylum claim before they "enter" the country. The creation of the legal fiction of "international zones" allows a state to remove the asylum-seeker without their having access to the state's jurisdiction. Both France and Germany have procedures of this type, which do not meet the essential requirements of a fair and satisfactory procedure.

"Safe third country"

Legislation in many countries in Western Europe and North America, as well as Australia, prevents refugees gaining asylum within these states by establishing the category of the "safe third country". While practices vary, these states do not consider the asylum claims of refugees deemed to have passed through another country on their way to the state in which they claim asylum. They argue that the"third country" (the country through which a refugee passed) is responsible for providing protection, without any regard to whether they will in fact get protection. Many asylum-seekers have been subjected to *refoulement* from third countries, and even from "fourth" or "fifth" countries. Chain deportation of asylum-seekers to countries where they may be persecuted is the result of states avoiding their responsibilities.

International refugee law does not require that a refugee must seek asylum in the first country whose territory he or she reaches. It is the country where a refugee applies for asylum which is obliged to consider the application substantively and to ensure that the refugee is not directly or indirectly returned to persecution. The only recognized exception to this principle is when the applicant has already found effective protection in another country, known as the "first country of asylum". Simply having been present in a country does not make it a first country of asylum.

EU states have implemented a number of policies which abuse the principle of "first country of asylum". Among them are the Schengen Supplementary Agreement and the Dublin Convention, both treaties that have been ratified by a number of European countries.[42] The effect of these treaties is that when an asylum-seeker's application is rejected by one European state, it will not be reconsidered by another.[43] The treaties also set out criteria to determine which state should be responsible for handling the application. For the many refugees who have to enter without the required travel documents and visas, that state will be the first that the refugee has entered, even if only in transit and regardless of where the refugee applies for asylum. The treaties assume — without any further guarantees — that all EU member states have fair and satisfactory asylum procedures and protect refugees against *refoulement*.

The treaties also explicitly allow asylum-seekers to be sent to third countries outside the EU. This was reinforced in 1992 when

EU Ministers for Immigration adopted a resolution on "host third countries" (countries which they intend to treat as if they were first countries of asylum). The definition of host third countries does not fulfil the criteria of first countries of asylum. The effect of the resolution is that EU states will identify whether there is a "host third country" before considering an asylum claim. In other words, if they can send an asylum-seeker elsewhere, they will. The decision on whether another state is a host third country is made by the EU state without asking the consent of the third country.

The result is that there is no guarantee that refugees seeking asylum in the EU will have access to a fair and satisfactory asylum procedure. They may be returned to a third country outside the EU without any guarantee that they will be admitted, will have access to a fair and satisfactory asylum procedure or will be protected against *refoulement*. Such "safe third country" practices have now been taken up by states outside the EU and violate the obligations all states have towards refugees.

In Australia, provisions introduced in 1994 on "safe third countries" were used to designate China as safe for all Vietnamese seeking asylum in Australia after previously being resettled in China, even though they expressed fear of being persecuted in China.

A state can only be released from its obligation to consider someone's asylum application substantively if that responsibility is assumed by a safe third country, and it must first establish that the third country is both safe and explicitly guarantees that it will take on the responsibility. Even when such guarantees can be obtained, an asylum-seeker who has compelling reasons to remain, such as established family links in the asylum country, should not be removed to another country.

Readmission

General agreements, such as those concerning readmission, which relate to the return of people who have entered a country in an irregular manner without the necessary authorization, are not in keeping with international legal standards for the rights of refugees. Explicit guarantees from countries of readmission must be obtained in each case, regardless of any existing agreements between the removing country and the destination country.

Mariam Azimi, an Afghan, is hiding in a church in Norway with her two young children because she fears being sent back to Pakistan, the country to which she originally fled.

Millions of other Afghans — a fifth of the country's population — have fled abroad to escape one of the worst human rights tragedies in history. The mass flight began in the 1980s as Soviet and Soviet-backed forces clashed with Afghan Islamist Mujahideen groups. Gross human rights violations were committed by all sides. By the end of 1989, more than three million Afghan refugees were believed to be in camps in Pakistan. A further two million were in Iran.

After the Soviet withdrawal from Afghanistan in 1989, many refugees returned home under UN-sponsored programs. The vast majority, however, remained in the camps. Although some returned in 1992, many subsequently left again for neighbouring countries when human rights abuses and inter-factional fighting intensified. They were joined by hundreds of thousands of others who fled the country for the first time. At least a million people have also been displaced inside Afghanistan.

The human rights catastrophe from which Afghans have fled has been the product of years of endemic violence, often fuelled by outside powers, combined with a lack of an effective central authority. Warring factions carry out deliberate artillery attacks on residential areas using weaponry supplied from abroad. Tens of thousands of women, men and children, the vast majority of them unarmed civilians, have been killed in such attacks since April 1992 when the Mujahideen forces took power. In 1996 the forces of one of the groups, Taleban, deliberately and indiscriminately attacked residential areas in and around the capital, Kabul, killing many civilians.

Other gross human rights violations are reported daily. They include deliberate and arbitrary killings, arbitrary detention, torture, including rape of women and children, and cruel, inhuman or degrading treatment and punishment of prisoners. Thousands of people have "disappeared" after being abducted by armed guards belonging to the various armed political groups.

Former detainees have testified they have been tied to dead bodies for days and forced to eat what they were told was human flesh. They have described how they were beaten with rifle butts, given electric shocks, suffocated to the point of near death, and had their testicles crushed with pliers. Young girls have been repeatedly raped in custody.

Those most at risk include members of specific ethnic, religious or political groups in areas controlled by warlords hostile to them, as well as those professing secular ideas, academics and other professionals, including journalists, and educated women such as Mariam.

Mariam was in particular danger because she used her education to campaign for women's rights. Her entirely peaceful activities forced her to flee not only Afghanistan, but also Pakistan, where

Mariam Azimi © Jon Bjørnsen 1996

she had initially sought sanctuary.

In the 1970s she was a leading member of the Revolutionary Association of Women of Afghanistan (RAWA), a left-wing organization opposed to the Soviet-backed Afghan Government as well as Afghanistan's armed Mujahideen groups. Many members of RAWA were assassinated. In the late 1980s and early 1990s she continued advocating women's rights in defiance of the increasingly dominant Mujahideen groups. After receiving repeated death threats, she fled to Pakistan.

There she continued promoting women's rights. Again, she was threatened by Afghan Mujahideen groups who continue to operate in border areas in Pakistan. Attempts were also made to kill members of her family living in Quetta, Pakistan. The Pakistani police have offered little protection to those targeted by Mujahideen groups. A leading member of RAWA, Mina Keshwar Kamal, who was known to be in danger in Pakistan, was raped and killed in her house in Quetta in 1987.

Mariam sought refuge in a Norwegian church after she was refused asylum on the grounds that it was safe for her to return to Pakistan.

Amnesty International urges all governments to ensure that no asylum-seekers are returned to Afghanistan, as no area of the country can be considered permanently safe, or to Pakistan if they fear abuses by Mujahideen groups. It also appeals to the international community to recognize its responsibility for the carnage in Afghanistan and to help find a solution to the ongoing human rights disaster. Only when the grave levels of human rights violations are brought to an end will the mass exodus of Afghans stop and a safe return of Afghan refugees be possible.

Refugees fleeing Kabul, capital of Afghanistan © Martin Adler/Panos Pictures

"Internal flight alternative"

States have developed other new notions to deflect responsibility
for refugees. One of these is the "internal flight alternative" — the
idea that a refugee can flee to a safe area within the country of origin and therefore does not need to seek asylum abroad. This "solution" has been used in many states as a basis for refusing asylum in
recent years.

The UN Refugee Convention does not explicitly deal with this
issue, although the OAU refugee definition protects those escaping serious disruption of public order "in either part or the whole"
of their country of origin.

The practical application by states of the "internal flight alternative" is usually in flagrant contravention of the UN Refugee Convention. Even if the human rights situation in a given area of a
country is stable (and states often rush to assume stability before it
has been securely established), an individual may have good
grounds for fearing persecution. The individual case must be considered on its merits. For example, someone wanted by the national
authorities as a subversive is unlikely to be safe, even in a part of
their home country where human rights violations are not the rule.
Many refugees have been sent back to countries such as India,
Somalia, Sri Lanka and Turkey without regard to their individual
grounds for fearing persecution, and without a proper assessment
of their safety during or after their return.

The interpretation of the "internal flight alternative" varies,
but countries of asylum often fail to take into account the individual circumstances of the asylum-seeker. In addition, the person
must be able to reach the area deemed safe — some people have
been sent back from Canada to areas of Somalia which could only
be reached by travelling through war zones where they would be at
serious risk.

No refugee should be returned to another area of their country of origin unless an examination of their individual case shows
that the human rights situation there is stable, that the individual
can safely reach the area of return, and that the individual will have
access to protection in the area. If any of these criteria cannot be
satisfied, there is no internal flight alternative.

6 Safe to return home?

"Temporary protection"

When hundreds of thousands of people fled the conflict that erupted in former Yugoslavia in 1991, European countries reacted by closing their borders and putting visa restrictions in place, claiming that they could not cope with this "mass influx". After interventions by UNHCR, Western European states then offered "temporary protection" to those fleeing. The convergence of politics and pragmatism had led UNHCR to advocate that the refugees be given "temporary protection" in Western Europe, instead of access to refugee determination procedures under the UN Refugee Convention. UNHCR was in the unenviable position of trying to convince states to keep their borders open and to respect the principle of *non-refoulement*, while seeking the cooperation of governments apparently more concerned with limiting the duration of protection than with guaranteeing its effectiveness.

A very different form of temporary protection had earlier been used in the case of people fleeing from Viet Nam and other southeast Asian countries in the 1980s. Under the Comprehensive Plan of Action (CPA)[44] for Indochinese refugees, countries in the region where refugees initially fled, such as Hong Kong, were given financial support to accommodate asylum-seekers while they were "screened" to decide if they were refugees. Those "screened in" would be resettled in other countries; those "screened out" would be repatriated. The commitment of the states of first asylum was limited to accommodating them in camps and detention centres until they could be resettled elsewhere. Between 1989 and 1995, some 80,000 Vietnamese people who had fled by sea were resettled outside the region and more than 72,000 were repatriated to Viet Nam.

There is no firm consensus at the international level as to what is meant by temporary protection. Its use in various regions shows that temporary protection can be a useful tool in situations of mass exodus, if combined with respect for *non-refoulement* and other basic rights, while the search for solutions through repatriation and

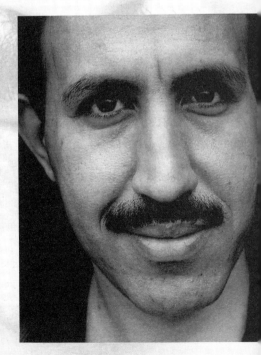

"I'm still haunted by a feeling of insecurity," says Idris, three years after he was granted asylum in the Netherlands. A 37-year-old Iraqi, he had spent most of the previous 10 years in detention or seeking refuge from human rights violations at the hands of the Iraqi authorities. During that time he narrowly escaped execution and survived prolonged periods of torture, before finally fleeing Iraq in 1993.

Like many new conscripts sent to the front during the Iran-Iraq war, he was so appalled by what he saw that he deserted. Shortly after he was arrested and held in a shipping container at the intelligence headquarters in Basra, where he was tortured.

On 7 April 1986 a number of army deserters were taken to a soccer stadium for execution. Idris lost consciousness and believes he was the only survivor. He regained consciousness in a van packed with dead bodies. It is a memory he cannot bear to describe. He was then sent back to his army unit where he deserted for a second time.

In August 1988 Idris was detained again and tortured with electric batons at various security and military installations. He was finally released from this nightmare in February 1991 after heavy bombardment in the area. Two years later his village was targeted for repeated house searches by the Iraqi military. Once again fearing for his life, Idris fled the country. Today he is studying engineering and says he is trying to rebuild his life "by a combined approach of forgetting and remembering".

resettlement is conducted.

The temporary protection model recently followed in Europe is based on the assumption that the people being given protection would eventually return home. European states were bound to respect the principle of *non-refoulement*, but in the face of what they saw as a mass influx of refugees they deemed it unnecessary to allow access to their individual asylum determination systems.

International refugee law does not give a right to permanent relocation. It provides only that refugees should be protected until they can return home in safety. Many states have in the past allowed refugees to remain permanently in their country, letting them integrate into their new community and rebuild their broken lives.

Now governments are turning to the concept of temporary protection at the same time as they are obstructing access to their countries, showing less and less respect for the principle of *non-refoulement*, and claiming that they cannot cope with the responsibility of sheltering refugees. They are using temporary protection as another means of denying refugees their rights.

People granted temporary protection are generally given fewer rights than those granted refugee status under the UN Refugee Convention. In the case of refugees from Bosnia, UNHCR stated in 1993 that almost all those fleeing would have qualified as refugees under the Convention.[45] Despite this, most were denied the chance of applying for refugee status and so denied their full range of rights under the Convention.

In addition, temporary protection can be ended by the host state far more easily than refugee status. The termination of refugee status requires that "a change of circumstances in a country is of such a profound and enduring nature that refugees from that country no longer require international protection, and can no longer continue to refuse to avail themselves of the protection of their country".[46] There is no such international standard for the termination of temporary protection, which means that states which host refugees on a temporary basis are not held accountable for the ending of temporary protection. Regardless of the duration of any protection, it is vital that internationally agreed human rights and refugee standards are complied with. In September 1996 Germany unilaterally decided to end the temporary protection status of Bosnian refugees, which opened the door for the forcible repatriation of people still frightened to go home and potentially at risk.

The concept of temporary protection rests on the idea that refugees will be able to return home safely, or resettle elsewhere, within a relatively short period. However, the history of refugee movements shows that the causes of flight are not easily remedied. For example, there are continuing grave human rights violations in Bosnia-Herzegovina. Yet states have proved unwilling to extend the "temporary protection" granted from 1992 onwards to refugees from there and have taken the signing of the Dayton peace agreement as a green light to start returning refugees. UNHCR has publicly "regretted" Germany's decision to allow forcible repatriation, but such decisions are beyond its control. In the December 1996 Humanitarian Issues Working Group Regional Plan, UNHCR put forward guidelines for returns to Bosnia-Herzegovina, insisting on individual screening procedures, but also indicating that some returns could be on a "less than voluntary basis".[47]

The reason European states gave for limiting the protection afforded to those fleeing former Yugoslavia was that this was a mass influx. There is no standard defining what constitutes a mass influx, but most European states outside the former Yugoslavia in fact admitted only a few thousand refugees from former Yugoslavia. Germany was the major exception, admitting more than 300,000. The response of European states to the flight from former Yugoslavia represents a watershed in the demise of the international refugee protection system, as states justified lessening protection based on a perceived threat to their national interests.

Mass movements of refugees have taken place frequently in other parts of the world. Under the OAU Convention and the Cartagena Declaration the definition of who is a refugee is broad, and allows for group determination of status. The protection offered is temporary in nature, based on the need to provide refuge to those who are in need of protection until they can return home.

While it may be accepted that temporary protection accorded to asylum-seekers in situations of mass exodus is a necessary and appropriate response by states faced with the prospect of hosting large numbers of refugees, this is only viable and responsible if this form of protection meets international refugee law and fundamental human rights standards.

The renewed use of temporary protection indicates a gap in the international refugee protection system — the inability to deal coherently with refugees fleeing as part of a mass exodus and the failure of the international community to share the responsibility for protecting such people. It also shows the inadequacy of the current international system to address in a consistent manner the fact that a growing number of people fall outside the narrow interpretation of the UN Refugee Convention definition of a refugee, yet cannot safely be returned to their countries of origin because of widespread human rights abuses, often associated with armed conflict.

Temporary protection undermines the standard of protection for asylum-seekers if they are forced to return to a country before basic human rights conditions in that country have been met. States have not yet agreed a set of practical, non-binding guidelines on when it is appropriate to use temporary protection, let alone standards on what rights those temporarily protected should enjoy in host countries. Amnesty International believes that if states unilaterally decide to use temporary protection, then standards should be agreed, based firmly on human rights considerations, and that all those offered temporary protection should have an opportunity to have their individual asylum claim examined before being sent home.

After the recent experience of the lifting of temporary protection in Europe, it is clear that political and institutional considerations can interfere in assessments of when it is safe and appropriate to end temporary protection. The ending of temporary protection, and any other form of refugee status, must be based on an evaluation of the human rights situation in the country of return that is impartial, politically independent and in keeping with the standards established under the cessation clauses[48] of the UN Refugee Convention.

Voluntary repatriation

Voluntary repatriation is seen by the international community as the most favoured of the "durable solutions" for refugees, which also include resettlement in a third country and integration in the host country. At a time when states are increasingly reluctant to host large numbers of refugees, the temptation appears to be to find ways of sending refugees home without securing proper

"[Guatemalan soldiers] killed my father, my mother, my brother, they killed everyone. They burned them. So I went to Mexico when I was small, but now, once again, they are massacring us [in Guatemala]..."

The refugee who spoke these words was one of a community of over 200 refugee families who had lived in exile in Mexico for many years. The families had only returned to Guatemala after their safety had been guaranteed. Yet on the first anniversary of their return, in October 1995, Guatemalan soldiers entered the community and killed 11 people, including eight-year-old Santiago Coc Pop. A soldier shot him in the wrist, then chased him and shot him again in the head and chest, killing him.

Between 1993 and 1995 almost 20,000 refugees went back to Guatemala from Mexico. Most were indigenous families who had fled in the early 1980s from a civil war and a brutal government counter-insurgency campaign which claimed the lives of tens of thousands of Guatemalans and wiped out hundreds of highland villages. Approximately one million people were internally displaced between 1979 and 1983, out of a population of little more than eight million, and hundreds of thousands took refuge outside the country.

The refugee communities in Mexico were well-organized. Their representatives negotiated an agreement with the Guatemalan Government for the collective return of refugees. The 1992 agreement recognized returnees' rights, guaranteed their safety and promised them access to land. It ensured UN, local and international monitoring of the return process.

One community of families that returned under this agreement lives on the Xamán estate (*finca*) in the municipality of Chisec, department of Alta Verapaz. Its 206 families are mostly indigenous people of Q'eqchi, Q'anjobal, Ixil, Mam and K'iché origin. The community cultivates cardamom spice.

On 5 October 1995, the community was preparing to celebrate the first anniversary of their new settlement. At approximately 11.30 am, a military patrol entered the community. Within hours, 11 people had been shot dead — including Santiago and another child — and 30 had been wounded.

The presence of armed soldiers in the community was highly provocative. About 200 members of the community gathered, a few shouting at the soldiers, others asking them to leave. There was a scuffle. A witness describes what happened next:

"The armed men at the head of the patrol raised their weapons and pointed at the people, I saw four of these men at the head of the patrol who had their weapons raised and were firing them. Three of them were firing automatic weapons directly at body height while the other on the extreme right fired at the ground."

Other soldiers then began to fire indiscriminately. Some people were shot dead as they lay wounded on the ground, others were shot in the back when they tried to run away. A witness stated:

"I was talking to my brother-in-law who was on the ground, I could see he was seri-

Soldiers from the "Rubelsanto" military barracks

Santiago Coc Pop's father leaning over the body of his dead son.

ously wounded. There he was laying on the ground and I watched as a soldier came to finish off those who had been wounded".

Investigations conducted by national and international organizations, including UN bodies, are unanimous in holding the soldiers responsible for the Xamán massacre. They discount government claims that the soldiers were provoked, that community members started the shooting or that community members were armed.

The refugee return program has slowed down dramatically since the massacre. Refugees have suffered years of harassment, threats and human rights violations by the Guatemalan armed forces and their allies. Senior military and government officials continue to this day to accuse members of these communities of supporting the armed opposition. The Xamán massacre may not have been planned, but the incursion by members of the army into the community was a deliberate act of intimidation that ended in tragedy.

guarantees that they will be safe once returned.

The thinking behind voluntary repatriation is based on assumptions that are not necessarily true, and the guidelines for when it is safe to send refugees home are inadequate. UNHCR, the body responsible for protecting refugees, is also charged with promoting voluntary repatriation. The two roles can involve conflicting interests and be subject to contradictory political agendas. As a result, voluntary repatriation schemes are fraught with danger for refugees.

One of the key assumptions is that all refugees want to go home. This is based on the idea that refugees put their lives on hold while in exile and that their original homes and communities still exist. For many refugees, this is simply not true. People who have been in exile for years, perhaps decades, adapt and rebuild their lives. They become part of their new communities, contributing their skills and forming deep relationships with those around them. Their children may know only the country of exile. Uprooting such people from their host countries can be devastating.

Many other refugees have nowhere to return to. Their communities may have disappeared as a result of war, "ethnic cleansing" or genocidal violence. Their homes may have been destroyed or usurped. The country may have been divided into a patchwork of territories controlled by armed forces hostile to particular ethnic groups.

Where voluntary repatriation is a suitable solution, certain key principles should be observed. In all cases, it must never violate or undermine the principle of *non-refoulement*. All voluntary repatriation schemes must therefore be assessed on the basis of whether the refugees would be at risk of persecution or human rights violations during or after return. Amnesty International believes that there should be evidence that the change in the situation they fled is of such a profound and enduring nature that the refugees no longer require international protection. Even when such conditions exist in general, individual refugees may still need international protection because of their particular circumstances and fears, and should therefore always be offered the opportunity for an individual assessment of their continued need for protection before being repatriated.

The reality is that the vast majority of repatriations are

spontaneous, as refugees are "pushed" or "pulled" to return, or become tired of waiting for assistance. They are pushed by host states who reduce or cut off aid, or make it impractical or dangerous for them to stay. They are pulled by inducements, such as promises of land or improved human rights guarantees in their home countries, which may turn out not to be genuine. They are driven to return by desperation, as months go by in temporary camps where little or no support is provided.

In EXCOM Conclusion 40, the role of UNHCR is described as "promoting, facilitating and coordinating voluntary repatriation". Facilitating voluntary repatriation implies helping refugees who wish to be returned. Promoting repatriation, however, implies a more pro-active role. UNHCR has to deal with the competing demands of host states and countries of origin, and, possibly, the international donor community. Some of these may be impatient to initiate repatriation on the basis of political and economic interests, rather than the safety of the refugees.

Much of the rhetoric about voluntary repatriation includes concepts such as the "right to return" and "measurements of safe return". However, the right to return does not oblige refugees to leave their sanctuaries, and the safety of return must be based on human rights standards and assessments of individual situations.

The three main criteria agreed internationally in relation to repatriation are:

- repatriation should be voluntary;
- UNHCR, governments and non-governmental organizations should have a joint role in repatriations;
- voluntary repatriation should be facilitated and promoted.

The principle of voluntariness is fundamental to repatriation, but as a standard it is open to manipulation. It is often falsely assumed, however, that if repatriation is voluntary, it must be safe. Of course, refugees should have a say as to when they will be repatriated. But there must be a solid foundation on which to make decisions about repatriation. Refugees are often the best judges as to when the conditions which forced them to flee have changed sufficiently to allow them to return home. It is therefore crucial that refugees have ready access to impartial, detailed information about the human rights situation in their country of origin.

Repatriation to a country where there are still serious human

Bamboo huts stretch out as far as the eye can see. Located in Jhapha district in eastern Nepal, they are home to around 90,000 refugees from southern Bhutan, most of whom fled their homes in 1991 and 1992.

Life in the UNHCR-run camps is tolerable thanks to the efforts of refugees like Mangala Sharma. At the age of 28, and mother of two young girls, she has become a refugee leader. Her activities have done much to build a spirit of self-reliance in the camps, which run their own committees, schools and workshops. "For the sake of the children we try to keep happy," she says. "But inside we are crying."

The mass exodus of Nepali-speaking people from Bhutan began in late 1990 after the authorities introduced a policy of national integration on the basis of northern Bhutanese traditions and culture (*driglam namza*). Demonstrations against policies perceived to be discriminatory against ethnic Nepali people led to a government crackdown. Soldiers raided homes and many people were arrested

and tortured. Girls and women were raped. Everyone lived in fear that they would be the next victim.

The authorities also put increasing pressure on many Nepali-speakers to "voluntarily" leave the country. "Every day they would come to tell me to write my application to migrate to Nepal," remembers Mangala.

She eventually fled to eastern Nepal after her brother, a political activist, was blacklisted by the government.

Determined to make the best of a bad situation, she set up an organization in the camp called Bhutanese Refugees, Aiding Victims of Violence. Run by the refugees themselves, it trains women in skills such as dressmaking. The money raised from selling the produce is used to buy food to supplement the meagre diet given to the refugees.

On one level Mangala is fulfilled. On another she is empty. "Being a refugee is so sad because you don't have a country," she says. "For us, Bhutan is our only country."

A Bhutanese refugee camp in Nepal.
© David Orr/Panos Pictures

rights problems could well lead to a further exodus or more human suffering. Just one example of the possible consequences of premature return was the case of Rohingya refugees from Myanmar (Burma). In 1991 around a quarter of a million Rohingyas fled gross and widespread human rights violations committed by the Burmese army and sought refuge in Bangladesh. The following year thousands were forced to repatriate, a move condemned by UNHCR as mass *refoulement*. In 1993 a repatriation agreement was signed by UNHCR and Myanmar, and later that year the Burmese authorities agreed to let UNHCR monitor the return. Throughout 1993 and 1994 there were reports of Bangladeshi officials using threats, intimidation, physical abuse, withholding of food rations and other methods to coerce repatriation. Under pressure from the Bangladeshi authorities, UNHCR then sped up the repatriation process and carried out a massive registration for voluntary repatriation. Many non-governmental organizations present on the ground stated that refugees did not understand that registration was associated with repatriation, and that they later believed they had no choice but to return to Myanmar.

Despite continued massive human rights violations in Myanmar, including some targeted specifically at Rohingyas, tens of thousands of Rohingya refugees repatriated. Many others fled the camps in Bangladesh to avoid repatriation, including around 20,000 in 1995, and sought refuge in other countries. Some of those who returned to Myanmar have since been forced to flee again.

Over the past few years UNHCR has assumed primary responsibility for voluntary repatriations. The results have been inconsistent. The Namibian repatriation in the early 1990s was generally seen as successful, as was the repatriation of Guatemalans from Mexico and Mozambicans from Malawi, Zimbabwe and elsewhere. Other major voluntary repatriations have had mixed results, including those involving the return of Afghans from Iran and Pakistan.

The situation of refugees in Central Africa starkly illustrates the fragile state of international refugee protection. A statement issued by the Tanzanian Government in early December, endorsed and co-signed by the UNHCR, declared that: "all Rwandese refugees in Tanzania are expected to return home by 31 December

The conflict that engulfed the former Yugoslavia has given rise to another, almost hidden, human tragedy. It is the plight of those fleeing the carnage, whose rights as refugees have often been flagrantly violated.

Jasmin,* a 32-year-old citizen of Bosnia-Herzegovina, was a former member of rebel Muslim forces in his country. Several months after he had been captured by the Army of Bosnia-Herzegovina and dragooned into their ranks, he deserted and fled to Slovenia through Croatia, hoping to reach relatives in Germany.

Slovenian officials arrested him for illegally crossing the border. Instead of offering him protection, they handed him over to the Croatian authorities, claiming Croatia was a "safe third country". Jasmin was then returned by the Croatian authorities to Bosnia-Herzegovina, where he was reportedly arrested, threatened with ill-treatment and charged with desertion. Both Slovenia and Croatia thus violated the UN Refugee Convention, which they have signed. Under the Convention, the Slovenian authorities should not have returned Jasmin to Croatia without ascertaining that he would not be returned to

Bosnian Muslims who had fled their villages rebuilding their homes in 1996. Some of the newly repaired houses have since been deliberately damaged or destroyed.
© Howard J. Davies

face danger in his home country.

Many thousands of refugees have suffered *refoulement* at the hands of the Croatian authorities. Some were reportedly ill-treated while in Croatia. In February 1995, for example, dozens of Muslim refugees in the Kuplensko camp were arrested. Some were beaten. Forty-six of them were then forcibly returned to an area of Bosnia-Herzegovina from which they had fled fearing for their lives.

Another case involved Hajra,* a 17-year-old Bosnian woman who had sought refuge in the Former Yugoslav Republic of Macedonia. On 28 May 1994 she was put on a train bound for the Federal Republic of Yugoslavia without any opportunity to appeal against her expulsion. She was so terrified of being returned to Bosnia by the Yugoslav authorities that she jumped from the moving train and was killed.

More than half a million refugees from Bosnia and Croatia remain in other republics of the former Yugoslavia. Many fear being sent back to areas where their lives may be endangered. In June 1995 some 4,000 male Serbian refugees of military age were forcibly returned from Serbia to Serb-controlled areas of Bosnia-Herzegovina and Croatia to be mobilized into Serbian armed forces there. Mirko Drljaèa, who had been a refugee in Serbia since 1993, was shot in the legs by Serb police when he tried to escape forcible conscription. Six months later he was reportedly still unable to walk and no police officer had been charged.

In August 1995 an even larger number of male refugees who had fled the Krajina region of Croatia when the Croatian Army took control of the area were reportedly arrested by Serbian police. Many were seized in refugee reception centres where they were waiting for their asylum applications to be processed. They were forcibly expelled to Serbian-held areas of Bosnia-Herzegovina, in breach of the principle of *non-refoulement*, and mobilized into the Serbian armed forces. Refugee conscripts were reportedly brutally ill-treated for having "betrayed the Serbian cause".

One reason so many refugees remain in areas still scarred by nationalist-inspired violence is the attitude of European governments, notably members of the European Union (EU). As the human rights crisis unfolded, EU governments rapidly imposed visa requirements on people from the former Yugoslavia which in practice made it extremely difficult for many to reach Western Europe.

Those who did reach EU countries were not granted refugee status, with its associated rights, but rather some form of temporary permission to remain. The precise nature of the temporary protection varied from state to state, but it generally allowed them to remain while suspending their right to pursue an individual claim for asylum.

Among those who have fled are people from areas that have not directly experienced armed conflict. Hundreds of thousands of young men from all parts of Serbia and Montenegro travelled abroad to avoid being forced to take part in a war they condemned. Many of these are ethnic Albanians from Kosovo province in Serbia, who have also felt the need to escape the increased arrests, beatings and harassment by police searching for weapons.

Since the November 1995 peace agreement for Bosnia-Herzegovina, pressure has been put on Bosnian refugees living in Europe and the republics neighbouring Bosnia-Herzegovina to return home voluntarily. At the time of writing, however, there are few places in Bosnia-Herzegovina where their safety can be assured, and none where a permanent state of safety is apparent.

* pseudonym

1996." Within a month of this statement, the majority of Tanzania's
estimated 540,000 Rwandese refugees had gone back to Rwanda.
Thousands attempted to flee to other countries in the region in
order to avoid return to Rwanda, but were forced back by the Tanzanian military. Voluntary repatriation was not at issue — refugees
who felt it was unsafe to return were not given any other options. It
was only after the vast majority of refugees had repatriated that
UNHCR publicly expressed the hope that Tanzania would institute
a screening procedure to evaluate the claims of those too fearful to
return — an expression of hope from the very agency with the international institutional mandate to remind the world's governments
of their duty not to forcibly repatriate refugees in need of international protection.

UNHCR is mandated to look at all refugee situations with a
view to encouraging the conditions for voluntary repatriation. This
raises several unanswered questions, particularly in today's world of
violent and protracted conflicts.[49] These point to an apparent
effort by governments to fundamentally shift UNHCR's focus from
protection to assistance.

In any voluntary repatriation program, UNHCR is also
charged with actively monitoring the situation of returnees in their
country of origin. However, it can only do this with the full agreement of the states concerned and can only do it properly if adequate resources are available. It is therefore vital that UNHCR and
other human rights monitoring bodies have appropriate access to
the relevant countries and that monitoring is incorporated into any
agreements between UNHCR and the governments concerned.

Promoting, facilitating and monitoring of voluntary repatriation is very different to providing legal protection to refugees in
countries of asylum. As UNHCR says, voluntary repatriation calls
for a "different set of protection tools".[50] However, there is as yet no
clear international agreement on what these should be. In an era
when the terms of protection are shifting under schemes such as
temporary protection, and when mass flows of refugees are fre-
quent, it is vital to be clear about the criteria for voluntary repatriation.

The UNHCR handbook on voluntary repatriation is not re-
assuring. Although it sets out the aspects of repatriation that must
be taken into account, it gives little real guidance on what standards

should be required when determining when it is safe to return. In fact, it appears to "promote" and "encourage" repatriation in unsatisfactory conditions. It even suggests that repatriation might be helpful to a peace process in a precarious situation. UNHCR is always in a potentially contradictory position when dealing with voluntary repatriations, and it should be remembered that UNHCR is essentially governed by its member states, each of which has its own political agenda.

The most fundamental consideration must be that the human rights situation in the country of origin has improved to a sufficient extent that refugees can reasonably be expected to return. This raises the question of who decides if such conditions are met and who should monitor the situation after the repatriation.

The main role of UNHCR should be to promote the principle of *non-refoulement* and the protection of refugees. As one agency, governed by member states, UNHCR should not be expected to be both the agent to promote voluntary repatriation as well as the agency to protect and assist the same population.

Today's world requires new approaches to repatriation quite different from those applied traditionally. In the past, repatriations usually involved refugees whose countries had recently achieved independence or changed to a democratic form of government. In the 1990s, the usual scenarios involve countries that have been riven by ethnic strife and civil war. For these, the process of reconciliation, if possible, will be long and arduous. Formal amnesties or human rights guarantees will be of little value to the returning refugee if they are not accompanied by the political will to put them into effect, and if they do not represent a genuine commitment by the people themselves to live together in peace. This is a political and social challenge that extends far beyond the resolution of a refugee problem and in some cases affects the continuing viability of the nation itself. Repatriation in these circumstances is therefore just one component of a long process that will require the mobilization of support and resources from many parts of the international community.[51]

The world needs to heed the call of UNHCR for international support. This support should involve human rights organizations and UN human rights monitors, who can help monitor the country of origin before, during and after a voluntary repatriation exercise is conducted. When assessing the "safety" of areas of possible voluntary return, or when monitoring areas to which refugees have returned, all those involved, including governments and UNHCR, should make use of human rights information already available. This includes thematic and country reports, as well as resolutions, of the Commission on Human Rights, and reports of the UN treaty bodies, such as the Committee Against Torture.

The present system of voluntary repatriation lacks clarity, particularly in relation to current refugee crises. At the same time the international community is adopting an increasingly restrictive posture towards asylum-seekers, and the international agency responsible for protecting refugees is under growing pressure from host governments to return refugees to their country of origin. The combination of these factors means there is great danger that people will be "voluntarily repatriated" to situations where their human rights are at risk. The concept of repatriation therefore needs to be re-examined and clear, comprehensive guidelines drawn up in line with human rights standards and with a clear emphasis on the importance of an independent, impartial and non-political process for deciding when it is appropriate for refugees to return. Respect for the principle of *non-refoulement* is paramount. Repatriation will continue to play a central role in international refugee protection, but it must be defined in terms that give human rights considerations the highest priority at every stage.

7 International cooperation

The first responsibility of the world's governments is to stop the human rights violations that force people to abandon their homes and communities. If the international community committed the necessary resources and political will to preventing human rights abuses, then many refugee crises and individual tragedies could be averted.

For years the international community refused to acknowledge that the Iraqi Government was systematically killing and torturing its citizens. Year after year, it ignored Amnesty International's reports and UN submissions documenting torture, extrajudicial executions and the "disappearance" of hundreds of thousands of people in the country. Even when 5,000 Kurdish women, men and children were slaughtered by chemical weapons in Halabja in 1988, the world's governments still did nothing. Perhaps if the Iraqi Government had been confronted earlier by the international community about human rights violations against its own citizens, the subsequent Gulf War and refugee crisis could have been avoided.

In the two years before genocide erupted in Rwanda, the UN's own human rights experts warned that unless states took determined action, mass killings would follow. The international community failed to heed these warnings, then, when the massacres started, withdrew the UN's troops. Since then, one refugee crisis has followed another, with millions of men, women and children suffering dislocation, terror, disease, starvation and death.

In some cases, powerful governments have fuelled conflicts in which human rights have been the first casualty. In countries such as Afghanistan they have supplied, armed and encouraged conflict, knowing that their allies were committing human rights abuses. Now they are doing little to help end the continuing violence.

Once a human rights tragedy is unfolding, the international community has a responsibility to protect refugees who flee from it.

States have agreed to international treaties, but too often these are ignored for the sake of political or economic expediency.

The international community is also obliged to ensure that the costs of refugee protection are properly shared, regardless of where refugees have fled. The Preamble to the UN Refugee Convention states:

> "...the grant of asylum may place unduly heavy burdens on certain countries, and... a satisfactory solution... cannot therefore be achieved without international cooperation."

The rich countries must share this responsibility. They should stop obstructing refugees from reaching their territory and ignoring the enormous logistical and economic strain that refugees can bring to countries with relatively few resources.

The very essence of refugee protection is that protecting the fundamental rights of refugees is the responsibility of the international community, given that their relationship with their own state has broken down. Yet those countries who are most able to provide protection host the fewest refugees. This is not just "an accident of geography" — wealthy states are actively and increasingly taking measures to keep refugees from their borders.

In her opening address to the October 1996 session of EXCOM, Sadako Ogata, the High Commissioner for Refugees, called again on the international community to cooperate more in sharing the responsibility for refugees:

> "It is increasingly evident that where burden-sharing fails, protection problems rise. The burdens are very unevenly divided, between and within continents. Germany hosts more Bosnian refugees than all other countries in Western Europe together...[In] Côte d'Ivoire and Guinea...[there are] regions where Liberian refugees outnumber the local population. The same is true in many other countries... I am very worried that appeals such as those by UNDP [UN Development Programme] and UNHCR to alleviate the huge environmental and other damages in eastern Zaire and western Tanzania, have gone largely unheeded."

When there is inadequate response to such appeals, or promises are not followed by action, refugees invariably suffer. The countries of Africa, a region previously known for its generosity towards refugees in extremely difficult circumstances, are now showing an alarming decline in their willingness to provide asylum. For years Iran lived up to its international responsibilities towards refugees. It still shelters over two million, more than any other country in the world. For years it appealed to the international community for financial help. For years its pleas were ignored. In the early 1990s its policies towards refugees changed, and today asylum-seekers face rapidly deteriorating living conditions in Iran, as well as *refoulement* and less than "voluntary" return.

UNHCR has repeatedly called on the international community for action, most emphatically in 1995.

"...the lack of tangible international solidarity has remained an obstacle to the positive development of the international refugee protection regime. Successive EXCOM Conclusions, endorsed by the General Assembly, have called for international solidarity and burden-sharing, enjoining all States to take an active part, in collaboration with UNHCR, in efforts to assist countries, in particular those with limited resources, that host large numbers of refugees and asylum seekers. It remains the shared responsibility of the international community to support the capacity of host States and to receive and protect refugees, including States lacking the necessary resources and those where domestic concerns, including anti-immigrant sentiment as well as social, economic, political and environmental concerns, militate against effective protection. Issues of national security are also increasingly relevant in this respect, particularly in regard to the political and related consequences of a prolonged stay of large groups of refugees."[52]

Essentially, the system for the international protection of refugees is only as good as its constituent elements — the individual states. But these are largely free to decide on what they will contribute. The system is therefore dependent on the vagaries of individual states' decisions when it comes to financial support for the massive humanitarian effort required to protect and assist refugees.

UNHCR's funding depends on an annual appeal. This has political ramifications as well as fiscal implications. UNHCR needs long-term financial stability and manifest political independence if it is properly to fulfil its mandate as a non-political protection and assistance organization. States should establish arrangements that

ensure adequate funding for the ongoing and emergency operations of UNHCR and its partner agencies. Otherwise, responsibility
sharing will remain a hollow aspiration. International solidarity is
not just about money, but without financial support it cannot be a
reality.

Even when states agree to provide funds for refugees, they frequently fail to provide the money they have promised. At the October 1995 EXCOM meeting the representative from Rwanda noted
that in January 1995, donors had pledged contributions of about
$1 billion, of which only 30 per cent had been paid.[53] The many
calls for assistance by states that host large numbers of refugees are
still going unheeded.

States should also share the responsibility of granting asylum.
This means not only living up to their duties towards those who
arrive at their borders, but also making more active use of resettlement programs. Why should the countries where refugees flee first
be expected to host them all, while other countries host relatively
few?

When states send refugees back to "safe third countries", con-
fine them to "safe havens" in the region of origin, or insist that they
seek sanctuary in the "first country of asylum", they are inverting
the concept of responsibility sharing. Responsibility sharing does
not mean states deflecting responsibility for refugee protection to
the first state that a refugee can reach. Even if richer states were to
share the costs — which they do not — refugees are people, not
commodities, and respect for their human rights demands more
than money.

The experience of the Comprehensive Plan of Action (CPA)
for Indochinese refugees illustrates how the attempts by the international community to share responsibility have so far failed to
overcome the fact that regions experience unevenly the weight of
protection. Under the CPA, countries of first asylum in Asia initially
agreed to take in asylum-seekers, allow them to remain temporarily
and to screen them to determine if they were refugees. Western
countries agreed to resettle those who were found to qualify as
refugees. Tens of thousands of refugees were resettled under the
program, but asylum-seekers were detained for years, often in
dreadful conditions, screening processes were widely criticized as
inadequate or unfair, and people "screened out" were forcibly

Piré Salyar, a 40-year-old Syrian Kurd, is one of millions of refugees around the world who have had to flee their homeland because of their ethnic origin. Now, after a long and distressing search for asylum, he can finally sleep at night feeling safe.

In the 1980s the Syrian secret police arrested him after he had written articles describing the persecution of Kurds in the country. He was interrogated and ill-treated. Then his wife, Ludmilla, was interrogated about his activities. Believing that they faced imminent imprisonment and torture, they decided to flee with their two children.

"We were not the only ones. I saw many Kurds fleeing Syrian cities... All Kurds who stand up for Kurdish national rights were insulted and mistreated by the security service."

Using forged passports, the family went to Turkey and then to Ukraine, Ludmilla's birthplace. The Soviet authorities told Piré that he could only stay if he abandoned his political activities, so they travelled to what was then Czechoslovakia. After six weeks their asylum claim was turned down, and they went to Austria. Once again their asylum claim was rejected.

"It was a shock for my wife and me... We did not know where we could go now... We told them all the problems we had in Syria but nevertheless we got a negative decision."

The couple turned in desperation to Amnesty International to help them through the Austrian appeals system. Finally, they were granted leave to stay in October 1992.

"Our life has changed," says Piré. "I attended a course in computer applications... My wife and I attended a course in German. My wife works for a big telecommunications company. The children go to school and all in all I can say that we are very happy to have a normal life."

repatriated, some violently.

Recently, the success of western countries in insulating themselves from refugees has meant that other parts of the world bear a
heightened responsibility for refugees. This has long been true in
terms of the north-south divide. Now it appears to be happening
within Europe, as refugees who cannot reach Western European
states are increasingly seeking asylum in Central and Eastern European states, many of which are in a much weaker position economically to provide adequate protection and support.

Every major refugee situation requires the cooperation of
states, international humanitarian agencies, non-governmental
organizations and, of course, the refugees themselves. It is vital to
refugees that there be international solidarity, cooperation and
responsibility for their protection and assistance. It is also fundamentally in the interests of all states that they solve refugee problems collaboratively. If they do not, refugee problems can become
refugee crises.

In late 1996 patterns of serious human rights abuses in eastern
Zaire gave way to armed rebellion and open war. Hundreds of thousands of refugees and displaced persons from Burundi, Rwanda
and Zaire itself, were thrown into desperate situations. If they fled
to Rwanda, an uncertain fate awaited them, given the continuing
violations of human rights being committed there. If they fled within Zaire, undisciplined armies were waging battle out of control. If
they went to Burundi, they faced mass killings. These crises were
neither inevitable nor without warning.

Speaking at the October 1995 EXCOM meeting, the representative from Tanzania described the situation in the Great Lakes
region of Central Africa:

> "Poor countries have been forced, by an accident of geogra-
> phy, to receive an enormous case-load of refugees exceeding
> two million people. Faithful to its record of hospitality in pro-
> viding sanctuary to successive waves of Mozambican, Angolan,
> Zimbabwean, Namibian and South African refugees fleeing
> colonial and racial oppression, the United Republic of Tanza-
> nia is at present hosting about 1.4 million refugees, mostly
> from Rwanda and Burundi."

He went on to note the serious strains that these numbers
placed on his country, especially on the environment and the social

and physical infrastructure. He stated that the instigators of the 1994 massacres in Rwanda and other "undesirable elements" had infiltrated the camps, preventing genuine refugees from returning home and frightening the Tanzanian population in the villages close to the camps. He said that the Tanzanian Government was willing to continue to seek solutions to the refugee crisis, but that:

> "[t]here is unfortunately a tendency for the international community, when dealing with the refugee crisis, to consider that the weaker countries of asylum should live up to their humanitarian obligations at the expense of their national rights and interests... Tanzania...appeals to donors to continue helping it fulfil its obligations, particularly in the area of repatriation."

The funding did not come and over the next few weeks the Tanzanian Government prevented refugees who were fleeing from Burundi from entering the country and sent some refugees back to Rwanda and Burundi. In late November 1996 the Tanzanian Government announced that within three weeks more than 500,000 Rwandese refugees would be repatriated. UNHCR found itself in the position of either standing back and seeing refugees forcibly expelled or making the choice of assisting in these returns. In what has become one of the most widely criticized decisions of UNHCR in recent years, UNHCR agreed to support the Tanzanian officials in returning refugees from the camps.

Zaire has also warned of the consequences of failing to assist countries of origin and host countries. Its representative stated in 1995 that:

> "International opinion always seems to forget that the refugee problem is basically the result of the situation in the countries of origin. The lack of consistency between humanitarian statements and the practice of the international community and the United Nations is increasingly frustrating for asylum countries... Zaire has the impression that the international community is of the opinion that, since Zaire has agreed to receive refugees, it has to continue to support them stoically regardless of the problems they cause."

He went on to underline the fatigue of his nation in waiting for international assistance commensurate with the gravity of the problem:

It took Marie and her mother three days to walk through the dense forest of eastern Zaire to reach the Rwandese border. The journey from Kahindo refugee camp was only 20 miles, but was fraught with danger. Twelve-year-old Marie and her mother were fleeing fighting that had broken out in October 1996 between Zairian rebel groups, Zairian government soldiers and Rwandan Hutu interahamwe militias. Marie's mother described the confusion: "Many people were wounded and shot dead. We don't know who was doing the shooting. There were lots of people with guns who had no uniform." Marie was wounded: a bullet shattered her jaw.

In the space of a few days, some 500,000 mainly Hutu refugees trekked back into Rwanda, the country they had fled two years earlier. In 1994 the refugees had escaped to Zaire when the Tutsi-dominated Rwandese Patriotic Front took over Rwanda after a campaign of mass killings in which as many as a million Tutsis were slaughtered. The refugee camps where they lived in eastern Zaire had been controlled by exiled former Rwandese government officials and their allied *interahamwe* militias — the people responsible for the 1994 genocide. The militias had been undergoing military training in and around the camps, had intimidated the refugee population and had extorted a "war tax" to support their efforts to reinvade Rwanda. "The *interahamwe* were trying to stop us from going back to Rwanda," said Marie's mother.

The fate of Marie and the other refugees who returned to Rwanda was uncertain, given the pattern of human rights violations that persisted there in late 1996. Government soldiers ejected 350 newly arrived sick and exhausted refugees from a Red Cross-run hospital near the border on 18 November, forcing them to walk further into Rwanda. Every day, people were being arrested on suspicion that they had been involved in the genocide; often there was no evidence against them. The judicial system was not functioning: 87,000 detainees were being held, with little prospect of being fairly tried, in conditions so appalling that survival was a matter of luck. There were also hundreds of killings by government soldiers during the year.

Despite the return of so many refugees to Rwanda, hundreds of thousands of men, women and children were still in mortal danger in eastern Zaire and neighbouring countries at the time of writing. They faced starvation, disease and continuing violence.

In Zaire, more than 750,000 Zairians were internally displaced as a result of the fighting between government troops and Zairian armed groups backed by the Rwandese Government. Many civilians were killed in the east of the country in October 1996. After the town of Bukavu fell to the rebels, journalists counted 82 bodies, including that of the Archbishop of Bukavu, who had publicly accused the rebels of being supported by the Rwandese Government. Ethnic tensions in the area had been increasing for years, exacerbated by repeated human rights violations by Zairian troops.

Tens of thousands of mainly Hutu refugees from Burundi were also living in eastern Zaire when the violence erupted. They had fled civil war and ethnic violence in Burundi, which had escalated ever since the October 1993 assassination of Burundi's first democratically elected president. Many were forced back to Burundi in late 1996 by Tutsi-led Zairian armed groups and handed over to Burundi government forces at the border. Hundreds of adult men who returned were then rounded up and killed by the Burundi security forces near the border or in the capital, Bujumbura.

In December 1996, the Tanzanian Government issued an ultimatum to 500,000-plus Rwandese refugees ordering them out of the country by the end of the year.

Rwandese refugees returning home from eastern Zaire in late 1996.

UNHCR endorsed the plan. Over the following weeks Tanzanian troops forcibly returned hundreds of thousands of men, women and children across the border. In addition, some refugees were returned to Burundi. On 10 January 1997, almost all of a group of 126 refugees forced to go back to Burundi were killed within hours or even moments of crossing the border.

Decades of misrule and organized mass atrocities have set populations against each other in the Great Lakes region. But the many disparate groups from Rwanda, Zaire and Burundi have one thing in common: they are in grave danger of human rights abuses, and they are not getting the protection they need and deserve from the international community.

"The incomprehensible lack of concern on the part of the international community in general and the United Nations in particular about the causes of the tragedies taking place, for example, in the countries of the Great Lakes region...borders on complicity and might pave the way for a drift towards exclusion and ethnic purification...

"Assistance to refugees therefore has to go hand in hand with increased international support for host countries, as well as with more effective preventive action and stronger international support for rapid repatriation in safety and dignity... The international community has read reports of serious situations but has not reacted as it should have done, and one tragedy has consequently followed another..."

One year later, hundreds of thousands of refugees were trapped in Zaire by military conflict and were dying without food or water.

Representatives from other African countries made similar pleas for assistance — there are over five million refugees in the continent, and more than three times that number of internally displaced people.

The actions of the governments of Zaire and Tanzania in forcibly returning many refugees to countries which have not yet become demonstrably safe flagrantly breach fundamental principles of refugee protection. However, it must be recognized that these states found themselves hosting large numbers of refugees in the face of fast-diminishing support from the international community.

International accountability

The existing system of refugee protection depends on the actions of individual states. There is no mechanism for ensuring that their actions are consistent or for holding states accountable if they fail to honour their obligations. Governments provide little information about how they treat refugees, even though the UN Refugee Convention requires states to report to UNHCR on the condition of refugees, implementation of the UN Refugee Convention and any laws relating to refugees. UNHCR issues general reports on the practices of states and their adherence to the UN Refugee Convention. However, its ability to report publicly its findings is seriously constrained by the fact that it can effectively only operate in countries with the permission of the government and it relies on the goodwill of major funding states. While UNHCR annually compiles reports on the legal protection of refugees by governments, these reports are not made public. The UN High Commissioner for Refugees issues general statements on violations of the principle of *non-refoulement*, but does not make specific reference to the governments involved.

Ultimately, states have a duty to uphold international human rights standards and to promote respect for human rights in the countries from which refugees flee. This is the basis of the international community's responsibility to pursue long-term solutions to current refugee problems — restoring the refugees' right to return home. The causes of the initial flight condition the nature of the flight, the degree and duration of international protection required, the prospects for achieving durable solutions and the external assistance needed. In all of this, international cooperation is required.

At present, lack of commitment by the international community towards refugees is causing further suffering to people who have suffered too much already. Governments must act at home and abroad to stop the human rights violations that cause refugees to flee. They must ensure that all refugees receive the protection they need and deserve. They must contribute more equitably to the cost of and the sheltering of refugees. To do any less is to break their own commitments to refugees and to betray millions of men, women and children who desperately need protection.

Conclusions and recommendations

Over the past decade widespread disregard for human rights has caused one refugee crisis after another. At the same time, the system devised to protect refugees has fallen into disarray, with states showing increasing reluctance to host refugees. Every day governments are violating the principle of *non-refoulement*, the fundamental basis of refugee protection. UNHCR, the agency set up to guarantee international protection for refugees, appears unable to ensure that states fulfil even their minimum obligations towards those forced to flee their country.

This report outlines why people flee, why they need protection and the system that should, but does not always, provide that protection. It demonstrates that refugee crises cannot be resolved unless the underlying human rights issues are addressed. Amnesty International therefore calls on all governments to take concrete measures to prevent human rights violations and to live up to their obligations under international law to protect the fundamental human rights of their citizens. It also urges all armed opposition groups to abide by the principles of international humanitarian law. If respect for human rights was universal, no one would be forced to flee their home in search of protection abroad.

One essential element in restoring respect for human rights in countries where abuses have been widespread is ending impunity. Amnesty International calls on all governments to end impunity by investigating reports of human rights violations and bringing those responsible to justice. This would be a major step towards breaking the cycle of violence and giving refugees the confidence to return home.

Amnesty International also believes that many armed conflicts that cause refugees to flee are fuelled by outside powers that supply arms, personnel and expertise to protagonists known to disregard human rights. It therefore calls on all governments to end transfers of equipment and training for military, security or police forces that

Vietnamese asylum-seekers in detention in Hong Kong in the early 1990s.
© Howard J. Davies

are used to commit or facilitate human rights abuses.

The international system to protect refugees is in crisis. Many people who deserve protection are falling through the net: denied access to asylum procedures; wrongly told they do not qualify as refugees; sent back to countries where they will not be safe. However, instead of enhancing refugee protection, governments are trying to restrict even further the definition of who qualifies for protection and the degree of protection they should receive. The stark reality is that governments, both individually and collectively, are unwilling to commit themselves to a greater degree of protection. This has led Amnesty International to conclude that this is not a time to call for bold new measures by the international community, such as the development of new international standards. Rather, it is a time to remind the world's governments of their existing obligations towards refugees and to urge them to ensure that these minimum standards are respected. Amnesty International calls on the international community to ensure that the full framework provided by international human rights law is applied to the protection of refugees.

Amnesty International believes that basic human rights principles provide an inviolable standard of protection for all people, regardless of asylum decisions made by individual states. The organization opposes the return of anyone to a situation where they may be at risk of execution, "disappearance", torture or imprisonment as a prisoner of conscience. This position is the basis of Amnesty International's intervention on behalf of refugees.

The main thrust of Amnesty International's work is to combat the human rights abuses that force so many people to flee their homes in terror. In its 1997 campaign on the human rights of refugees, Amnesty International is focusing on the way governments treat refugees. The following recommendations outline the minimum steps necessary to protect the human rights of refugees so that they are safe from further harm and are treated with the dignity that their tragic circumstances demand.

To governments in countries of asylum

People usually become refugees because their human rights are at grave risk. They sever the link with their own state, and seek the protection of another state, because their own government is persecuting them or cannot be relied on to protect them. When refugees seek the protection of another state, they rarely receive a warm welcome. Many are turned back at the border without a hearing; detained as "illegal immigrants"; subjected to further violence or squalid conditions in refugee camps; put through summary and unfair asylum procedures; or sent back to the country they fled. Amnesty International urges governments in countries of asylum to:

1. Build awareness and public support for the rights of refugees

Governments in countries of asylum often obscure the relationship between human rights violations and the protection needs of refugees. As the number of those seeking protection increases, governments seem less willing to live up to their international obligations. Many governments which have offered people asylum in the past are now restricting access to their countries, often justifying such actions on the grounds that they are responding to economic difficulties or anti-immigrant attitudes and growing xenophobia within their societies.

● Host countries should conduct public information campaigns drawing attention to the human rights concerns underlying the plight of refugees and the obligations of states to protect them.

2. Ratify and implement international treaties

Ratification of international treaties relating to the protection of human rights and the rights of refugees demonstrates states' commitment to the values endorsed by the international community and allows them to be held accountable for their actions.

● All states should accede to and implement the 1951 Convention relating to the Status of Refugees (the UN Refugee Convention) and its 1967 Protocol, as well as relevant additional regional refugee treaties. They should also accede to and implement international and regional human rights treaties, including in particular the International Covenant on Civil and Political Rights (ICCPR); the International Covenant on Economic, Social and Cultural Rights (ICESCR); and the Convention Against Torture and Other Cruel, Inhuman or Degrading Treatment or Punishment (Convention Against Torture).

● All states that have declared reservations to the UN Refugee Convention, or maintain a geographical limitation incompatible with the intention of the 1967 Protocol, should withdraw them and extend the scope of protection to all refugees.

● All states should apply the full range of refugee and human rights treaties in determining who is entitled to protection as a refugee. Their assessment of claims should be based on international and regional refugee instruments and relevant human rights instruments.

3. Stop forcibly returning refugees to countries where they are at risk of serious human rights violations

The fundamental basis of international refugee law is the established principle of *non-refoulement*. This prohibits states from sending anyone against their will to a country where they would be at risk of serious human rights violations. It is a norm of customary international law, binding on all states irrespective of whether they are party to the UN Refugee Convention, and states cannot derogate from it. Other international human rights instruments also prohibit *refoulement* in all cases where a person would be at risk of serious human rights violations.

● States must scrupulously observe the principle of *non-refoulement*, and not forcibly return refugees, in any manner whatsoever (including rejection at the frontier and interdiction at sea), to frontiers of territories where they may face serious human rights violations.

● States should adhere to the full range of other international human rights standards so that no one is sent back to a situation where they may face grave human rights violations, such as torture, "disappearance" or execution.

● States should ensure that all asylum-seekers are referred to an independent and specialized body responsible for deciding asylum claims. Border officials should never decide claims; they should be instructed to refer each asylum-seeker to the responsible body.

● States should ensure that the principle of *non-refoulement* applies irrespective of whether an asylum-seeker has been formally granted refugee status.

● States should not penalize asylum-seekers for illegal entry.

● States should not interpret the term "coming directly" in

Article 31 of the UN Refugee Convention in a manner that excludes refugees who merely travel through another country before applying for asylum.

4. End practices that prevent or deter asylum-seekers pursuing claims

Article 14.1 of the Universal Declaration of Human Rights states that "everyone has the right to seek and to enjoy asylum from persecution". While governments are entitled to control immigration and entry to their territory, they should ensure that asylum-seekers have access to a fair and satisfactory asylum procedure. They should ensure that there are no restrictions on entry or border control measures that in practice obstruct access. They should not detain asylum-seekers in violation of international law. They should not deny asylum-seekers the means of adequate subsistence while their asylum claims are being considered, which can in practice force refugees to withdraw their claims because they cannot survive.

● States should ensure that any restrictive measures, such as visa controls, carrier sanctions and interdictive border controls, do not in effect prevent asylum-seekers obtaining access to their jurisdiction or asylum procedures.

● All asylum-seekers, in whatever manner they arrive at the border or within the jurisdiction of a state, must be referred to the body responsible for deciding asylum claims.

● Detention of asylum-seekers should normally be avoided. No asylum-seeker should be detained unless it has been established that detention is necessary, is lawful and complies with one of the grounds recognized as legitimate by international standards. In all cases, detention should not last longer than is strictly necessary. All asylum-seekers should be given adequate opportunity to have their detention reviewed by a judicial or similar authority.

● Governments should never detain asylum-seekers in order to deter people from seeking asylum in their country, to impede their asylum claim or to induce them to abandon their claim.

● Governments should not deny asylum-seekers access to adequate means of subsistence while their asylum application and any appeal is being considered.

5. Provide refugees with a fair and satisfactory asylum procedure
A fair and satisfactory asylum procedure is the only effective way to ensure that people who would be at risk of serious human rights violations if returned to a particular country are identified and offered protection.

- In each state, the body responsible for deciding asylum claims must be independent and specialized, with sole and exclusive responsibility for dealing with such claims. The decision-makers must have expertise in international human rights and refugee law. Their status and tenure should encourage the strongest possible guarantees of their competence, impartiality and independence. Decision-makers should be provided with objective and independent information about the human rights situation in asylum-seekers' countries of origin or any countries to which they might be sent.
- Asylum applicants should have the opportunity to be heard in person by the decision-maker when their claim is examined in the first instance. There should be an individual and thorough examination of all the circumstances of each case. Applicants should have adequate time to prepare their case.
- At all stages of asylum and related procedures, including expulsion or detention hearings, an asylum-seeker should have the right to legal counsel, be notified of that right, have access to qualified interpreters, and have the right to contact UNHCR and relevant non-governmental organizations.
- Asylum-seekers should be given, in a language they fully understand, the necessary guidance about the procedures to be followed and full information about their procedural rights.
- If their claim is initially rejected, they should be given the reasons for the decision in writing, in a language they fully understand, so that they can pursue satisfactorily any appeals.
- Every asylum-seeker must have the right to appeal. Appeals should normally be of a judicial nature and heard by a different body than that which heard the case in the first instance. An appeal should include a full examination of the case given the gravity of the interests at stake.
- All asylum-seekers must be allowed to stay in the host country during the asylum determination procedure, including

any appeals.

● All officials and procedures dealing with asylum-seekers should take into consideration the special situation of refugees. It is not always possible for an asylum-seeker to "prove" every part of her or his case. If an asylum-seeker's account is credible, she or he should be given the benefit of the doubt, unless there are good reasons to the contrary.

6. Accept responsibility for examining asylum claims

Increasing numbers of governments are avoiding their responsibility for examining asylum claims or transferring it to other countries. They use "safe third country" practices, measures such as "white lists" which exclude asylum-seekers based on the presumption that the country they fled is safe, readmission agreements between states which lead to the automatic return of people from one country to another, temporary protection schemes or other measures where the substance of the claim is not adequately assessed.

● The state in which an asylum-seeker lodges an asylum claim should normally assume responsibility for substantively examining that claim.

● All "safe third country" practices and similar bilateral and multilateral arrangements that allow asylum-seekers to be sent to a country where they would be at risk of direct or indirect *refoulement* or serious human rights violations should be ended immediately.

● Governments should not transfer their responsibility for examining an asylum claim to a third state unless they have received explicit consent that the refugee will be admitted and explicit guarantees that the applicant's claim will be examined in a fair and satisfactory asylum procedure and that the asylum-seeker will not be subject to *refoulement*.

● Procedures for dealing with claims presumed to be "manifestly unfounded" or submitted by asylum-seekers from countries presumed to be safe should offer the opportunity for a thorough and substantive examination of the claim using fair and satisfactory methods.

● While temporary protection schemes, or the granting of *de facto* or some form of humanitarian status, may sometimes provide interim protection, they should not be used to deny asylum-seekers access to a determination of the substance of their claim under the UN Refugee Convention. All those who are granted some form of interim protection must be given an opportunity to have their individual asylum claim assessed in a fair and satisfactory procedure, to determine if they are still in need of protection, before a decision is made to remove them from the country of asylum.

7. Recognize and meet the special needs of particular groups of asylum-seekers

Certain categories of asylum-seekers have special protection concerns due to their particular vulnerability or circumstances. For example, the protection needs of women, children and those persecuted because of their sexual orientation are often misunderstood or wrongly interpreted.

- All states should, as a minimum, adopt and implement the recommendations of the UNHCR Guidelines on the Protection of Refugee Women and the numerous EXCOM Conclusions concerning refugee women. These recognize and address the particular concerns of women while in flight, in camps and during asylum determination procedures.
- Governments should recognize that women may be forced to flee as a result of persecution in the form of sexual violence or other gender-related abuses, as acknowledged by the world's governments in the Beijing Declaration and Platform for Action adopted in 1995. Governments should ensure that asylum decision-makers understand that sexual violence and other gender-related abuses can constitute persecution under the UN Refugee Convention definition of a refugee.
- Governments should offer protection to women who fear persecution because they will not conform to, or have transgressed, gender-discriminating religious or customary laws or practices of their society. Governments should recognize that asylum claims on these grounds fall within the ambit of the UN Refugee Convention and international human rights instruments.
- Governments should take measures, including following guidance issued by UNHCR, to address the special protection needs of unaccompanied minors and of children in their own right. States should also implement the provisions of the Con-

vention on the Rights of the Child relating to children seeking refugee status.

● Governments should recognize that those persecuted because of their sexual orientation should be given protection under the UN Refugee Convention.

8. Protect the rights of refugees in situations of mass exodus

Mass human rights violations cause mass exodus. In some circumstances, when hundreds of thousands of people flee their country, governments may not be in a position to examine every individual case, but will grant asylum to the whole group. In effect, there is a *prima facie* presumption of refugee status. Before any person who has been part of a mass exodus is returned to the country they fled, they should be given an opportunity to identify themselves as having individual grounds for continuing to fear persecution if returned.

● States should explicitly endorse the fundamental obligations established in EXCOM Conclusion 22:

(i) In situations of mass exodus asylum-seekers should be admitted to the state where they first seek refuge. If that state is unable to admit them on a long-term basis it should always admit them on at least a temporary basis pending arrangements for a durable solution. In all cases the fundamental principle of *non-refoulement*, including non-rejection at the frontier, must be observed scrupulously.

(ii) Asylum-seekers in mass exodus situations should not be penalized or treated unfavourably solely on the grounds that their presence in the country is considered unlawful. They should not be subjected to restrictions on their movements except those which are necessary in the interest of public health and public order.

(iii) States where large groups of refugees seek asylum should respect the refugees' fundamental civil rights and should ensure that they have the basic necessities of life. The refugees should not be subjected to cruel, inhuman or degrading treatment and should not suffer discrimination.

(iv) States should provide the means for asylum-seekers to stay in a place of safety. This should not be close to dangerous border areas.

(v) All governments should provide effective assistance,

including financial support and resettlement opportunities, to states that host large numbers of refugees, for as long as it is required.

● Governments, in consultation with UNHCR and non-governmental organizations, should agree standards for the use of temporary protection schemes in situations of mass exodus. Such temporary protection schemes should not be used by states to undermine existing standards under the UN Refugee Convention.

● Governments should ensure that all those given temporary protection have the right to have their individual case for asylum examined before they are removed from the host country.

To the international community

Refugees have been forced to sever the bond with their own state and therefore have an exceptional status — they are of international concern. A special UN agency, UNHCR, was established to protect them and to provide them with assistance. However, at the international level, there is no coordinated scrutiny or monitoring of refugee protection, and considerations other than human rights often drive refugee policies. The crisis in refugee protection and related human rights issues are not being addressed in a comprehensive way. Amnesty International urges the international community to:

9. Base repatriation programs on human rights standards

The internationally agreed standard on repatriation states that "the voluntary and individual character of repatriation and the need for it to be carried out under conditions of absolute safety...should always be respected." Recent experience shows that many repatriations are not genuinely voluntary; rather there is premature, forced and coerced return to less than safe conditions. Equally fundamental to any decision that a refugee can repatriate is an assessment of their safety upon return, measured according to human rights standards. Any decision on repatriation should be based on an independent, impartial and objective assessment of the human rights situation in the country of return, with a view to the durability of that safety.

● The principle of *non-refoulement* must never be violated by repatriation schemes. Repatriation programs should include human rights guarantees at all stages of the return. Repatriation should not be imposed until there is a fundamental and lasting change in the human rights situation in the country of return.

● The human rights situation in the country of return should be subject to independent and impartial assessment based on publicly available information before, during and after any repatriation. International human rights treaty bodies, thematic mechanisms and country rapporteurs should have an active role in this assessment.

● The international community, including governments, international organizations and non-governmental organizations, should immediately agree on how to provide an independent human rights assessment and monitoring system for repatriation programs. They should determine what type of organizations and agencies should be involved on an ongoing basis.

● Efforts should be made to ensure the involvement of a representative cross-section of the refugee community in assessing when return is possible.

● Governments in countries from which refugees have fled should cooperate with UNHCR, other international organizations, and non-governmental human rights and humanitarian organizations in the pursuit of durable solutions to refugee problems. They should allow access to their countries so that the human rights situation can be properly assessed throughout any repatriation program.

● Individuals should have the right not to repatriate without an adequate opportunity for an individual assessment of their asylum claim.

● When refugees are repatriating spontaneously rather than as part of an organized program, governments, UNHCR and other agencies should continue to exercise responsibility for ensuring that refugees are not put under undue pressure to return, and that measures are taken to ensure the safety of returning refugees.

10. Strengthen international solidarity and responsibility sharing
All states should share equitably the responsibility for hosting refugees and funding their support. States should not bear a dis-

proportionate share of the responsibility simply because of their geographic location. States hosting refugees should receive the full support of the international community. International organizations responsible for providing refugee protection and assistance should be able to operate without political interference by governments and with secure funding.

- UNHCR funding arrangements should urgently be reviewed to create an adequate mechanism for funding ongoing programs and, in particular, to improve the support for those states which bear the overwhelming responsibility for hosting refugees.
- UNHCR should be enabled to implement in full its protection mandate in a consistent manner and should be shielded from the political agendas of donor countries.
- "Responsibility sharing" should not be used to prevent refugees from seeking asylum in the country of their choice or to limit protection to the region of origin. All countries should share the responsibility for hosting refugees by making re-settlement — one of the "durable solutions" — a viable option.

11. Make the international system more accountable

At present little information is provided by governments about the protection they offer refugees and how they apply international refugee law. This makes it more difficult to hold governments to account if they fail to live up to their obligations towards refugees.

- States should comply with their reporting obligations under the UN Refugee Convention. UNHCR should submit these reports to the UN General Assembly annually.
- An independent, impartial mechanism should be established to monitor the compliance of States Parties to the UN Refugee Convention and its 1967 Protocol.

12. Ensure that internally displaced people are protected

Millions of people have fled from the risk of human rights abuses but have not crossed an international border. Indeed, many people have been prevented from leaving their country as a result of efforts by other governments to restrict access to their countries. While the internally displaced often flee for the same reasons as asylum-seekers who have fled to other countries, only people outside their country of origin can receive international protection as refugees. The discrepancy between the protection accorded to refugees outside their country and the lack of protection for those who are internally displaced should receive greater international attention and concern. The issue of the protection and assistance needs of the internally displaced is especially urgent in view of the increased number of such people in many parts of the world and their particular vulnerability to gross human rights abuses.

● Measures taken by the international community for the protection of internally displaced people should not limit their right to seek and to enjoy asylum in other countries.

● All states should support the work of the Representative for Internally Displaced Persons of the UN Secretary-General by allowing access to their countries and by providing adequate resources. The role of the Representative should be strengthened to enable the Representative to identify perpetrators of human rights abuses against internally displaced people so as to ensure that they are held to account.

● The international community should take concrete measures to ensure that internally displaced people are protected. The Representative should develop guidelines for the protection of internally displaced people, based on the full range of existing human rights and humanitarian law, addressing any current gaps in the protection of internally displaced people.

● Governments and armed opposition groups in control of territory should allow access to displaced people to relevant UN, intergovernmental and non-governmental organizations working on behalf of the internally displaced.

APPENDIX I
International and regional refugee standards

1951 United Nations Convention relating to the Status of Refugees and its 1967 Protocol relating to the Status of Refugees

States which have ratified or acceded to a convention are party to the treaty and are bound to observe its provisions. States which have signed but not yet ratified have expressed their intention to become a party at some future date; meanwhile they are obliged to refrain from acts which would defeat the object and purpose of the treaty.

(As of 19 February 1997)

	Convention relating to the Status of Refugees (1951)	Protocol relating to the Status of Refugees (1967)
Afghanistan		
Albania	x	x
Algeria	x	x
Andorra		
Angola	x	x
Antigua and Barbuda	x	x
Argentina	x	x
Armenia	x	x
Australia	x	x
Austria	x	x

	Convention relating to the Status of Refugees (1951)	Protocol relating to the Status of Refugees (1967)
Azerbaijan	x	x
Bahamas	x	x
Bahrain		
Bangladesh		
Barbados		
Belarus		
Belgium	x	x
Belize	x	x
Benin	x	x
Bhutan		
Bolivia	x	x
Bosnia and Herzegovina	x	x
Botswana	x	x
Brazil	x	x
Brunei Darussalam		
Bulgaria	x	x
Burkina Faso	x	x
Burundi	x	x
Cambodia	x	x
Cameroon	x	x
Canada	x	x
Cape Verde		x
Central African Republic	x	x
Chad	x	x

	Convention relating to the Status of Refugees (1951)	Protocol relating to the Status of Refugees (1967)
Chile	x	x
China ·	x	x
Colombia	x	x
Comoros		
Congo	x	x
Costa Rica	x	x
Côte d'Ivoirea	x	x
Croatia		
Cuba		
Cyprus	x	x
Czech Republic	x	x
Denmark	x	x
Djibouti	x	x
Dominica	x	x
Dominican Republic	x	x
Ecuador	x	x
Egypt	x	x
El Salvador	x	x
Equatorial Guinea	x	x
Eritrea		
Estonia	x	x
Ethiopia	x	x
Fiji	x	x
Finland	x	x

	Convention relating to the Status of Refugees (1951)	Protocol relating to the Status of Refugees (1967)
France	x	x
Gabon	x	x
Gambia	x	x
Georgia	x	x
Germany	x	x
Ghana	x	x
Greece	x	x
Grenada		
Guatemala	x	x
Guinea	x	x
Guinea-Bissau	x	x
Guyana		
Haiti	x	x
Holy See	x	x
Honduras	x	x
Hungary	x	x
Iceland	x	x
India		
Indonesia		
Iran (Islamic Republic of)	x	x
Iraq		
Ireland	x	x
Israel	x	x
Italy	x	x

	Convention relating to the Status of Refugees (1951)	Protocol relating to the Status of Refugees (1967)
Jamaica	x	x
Japan	x	x
Jordan		
Kazakstan		
Kenya	x	x
Kiribati		
Korea (Democratic People's Republic of)		
Korea (Republic of)	x	x
Kuwait		
Kyrgyzstan	x	x
Lao People's Democratic Republic		
Latvia		
Lebanon		
Lesotho	x	x
Liberia	x	x
Libyan arab Jamahiriya		
Liechtenstein	x	x
Lithuania	x	x
Luxembourg	x	x
Macedonia (former Yugoslav Republic of)	x	x
Madagascar	x	

	Convention relating to the Status of Refugees (1951)	Protocol relating to the Status of Refugees (1967)
Malawi	x	x
Malaysia		
Maldives		
Mali	x	x
Malta		
Marshall Islands		
Mauritania	x	x
Mauritius		
Mexico		
Micronesia (Federated States of)		
Moldova		
Monaco	x	
Mongolia		
Morocco	x	x
Mozambique	x	x
Myanmar		
Namibia	x	
Nauru		
Nepal		
Netherlands	x	x
New Zealand	x	x
Nicaragua	x	x
Niger	x	x

	Convention relating to the Status of Refugees (1951)	Protocol relating to the Status of Refugees (1967)
Nigeria	x	x
Norway	x	x
Oman		
Pakistan		
Palau		
Panama	x	x
Papua New Guinea	x	x
Paraguay	x	x
Peru	x	x
Philippines	x	x
Poland	x	x
Portugal	x	x
Qatar		
Romania	x	x
Russian Federation	x	x
Rwanda	x	x
Saint Kitts and Nevis		
Saint Lucia		
Saint Vincent and the Grenadines	x	
Samoa	x	x
San Marino		
Sao Tome and Principe	x	x
Saudi Arabia		

	Convention relating to the Status of Refugees (1951)	Protocol relating to the Status of Refugees (1967)
Senegal	x	x
Seychelles	x	x
Sierra Leone	x	x
Singapore		
Slovak Republic	x	x
Slovenia	x	x
Solomon Islands	x	x
Somalia	x	x
South Africa	x	x
Spain	x	x
Sri Lanka		
Sudan	x	x
Suriname	x	x
Swaziland		x
Sweden	x	x
Switzerland	x	x
Syrian Arab Republic		
Tajikistan	x	x
Tanzania	x	x
Thailand		
Togo	x	x
Tonga		
Trinidad and Tobago		
Tunisia	x	x

	Convention relating to the Status of Refugees (1951)	Protocol relating to the Status of Refugees (1967)
Turkey	x	x
Turkmenistan		
Tuvalu	x	x
Uganda	x	x
Ukraine		
United Arab Emirates		
United Kingdom	x	x
United States of America		x
Uruguay	x	x
Uzbekistan		
Vanuatu		
Venezuela		x
Viet Nam		
Yemen	x	x
Yugoslavia (Federal Republic of)	x	x
Zaire	x	x
Zambia	x	x
Zimbabwe	x	x

x — denotes that country is a party, either through ratification, accession or succession

Geographical limitation
Article 1 B(1) of the 1951 Convention provides: "For the purposes of this Convention, the words 'events occurring before 1 January 1951' in article 1, Section A, shall be understood to mean either:
(a) 'events occurring in Europe before 1 January 1951'; or
(b) 'events occurring in Europe or elsewhere before 1 January 1951',
and each Contracting State shall make a declaration at the time of signature, ratification or accession, specifying which of these meanings it applies for the purposes of its obligations under this Convention. The following States adopted

alternative (a), the geographical limitation:
Congo, Madagascar, Monaco, Hungary, Malta and Turkey.

    Hungary, Malta and Turkey expressly maintained their declarations of geographical limitation upon acceding to the 1967 Protocol. Madagascar and Monaco have not yet adhered to the Protocol. All other States Parties ratified, acceded or succeeded to the Convention without a geographical limitation by selecting option (b).

Source: UNHCR

Parties to the OAU Convention

(*indicates state which has signed but not ratified)

Algeria	Gambia	Nigeria
Angola	Ghana	Rwanda
Benin	Guinea	Senegal
Botswana*	Guinea-Bissau	Seychelles
Burkina Faso	Kenya*	Sierra Leone
Burundi	Lesotho	Somalia
Cameroon	Liberia	Sudan
Cape Verde	Libya	Swaziland
Central African Rep.	Madagascar*	Tanzania
Chad	Malawi	Togo
Congo	Mali	Tunisia
Côte d'Ivoire*	Mauritania	Uganda
Egypt	Mauritius*	Zaire
Equatorial Guinea	Morocco	Zambia
Ethiopia	Mozambique	Zimbabwe
Gabon	Niger	

Member States of the OAS

(*indicates original presenter of Cartagena Declaration)

Antigua & Barbuda	Dominican Rep.	Peru
Argentina	Ecuador	St Christopher
Bahamas	El Salvador*	& Nevis
Barbados	Grenada	St Lucia
Belize*	Guatemala*	St Vincent & the
Bolivia	Guyana	Grenadines
Brazil	Haiti	Suriname
Canada	Honduras*	Trinidad &
Chile	Jamaica	Tobago
Colombia*	Mexico*	United States
Costa Rica*	Nicaragua*	Uruguay
Cuba	Panama*	Venezuela*
Dominica	Paraguay	

(The Cartagena Declaration is not a legally binding treaty)

APPENDIX II
The UN High Commissioner for Refugees and its Executive Committee

UNHCR

The United Nations High Commissioner for Refugees (UNHCR) was established in 1950 as a humanitarian and non-political organization which deals with and attempts to find solutions for the problems of refugees. UNHCR's Statute details two facets of its work: providing international protection for refugees and seeking permanent solutions for their problems. The organization also works on behalf of people who are fleeing from armed conflict and human rights violations and has, in recent years, begun to assist people who are displaced within their own country. It is funded by voluntary contributions (both monetary and in-kind) from governments, intergovernmental organizations and non-governmental organizations.

UNHCR's Statute defines a refugee in almost exactly the same terms as the UN Refugee Convention. Over the years, however, it has been asked by the international community to take responsibility for groups of refugees who fall outside that original definition. In practice, therefore, the definition applied by UNHCR when recognizing refugees under its original mandate is wider than the definition as written in the Statute.

EXCOM

The work of UNHCR is overseen by its Executive Committee (EXCOM), which is comprised of representatives of 51 states from all over the world who are particularly involved in refugee matters.

Current EXCOM member states

Algeria	Hungary	Philippines
Argentina	India	Russian Federation
Australia	Iran	Somalia
Austria	Ireland	Spain
Bangladesh	Israel	Sudan
Belgium	Italy	Sweden
Brazil	Japan	Switzerland
Canada	Lebanon	Tanzania
China	Lesotho	Thailand
Colombia	Madagascar	Tunisia
Denmark	Morocco	Turkey
Ethiopia	Namibia	Uganda
Finland	Netherlands	United Kingdom
France	Nicaragua	United States
Germany	Nigeria	Venezuela
Greece	Norway	Yugoslavia
Holy See	Pakistan	Zaire

EXCOM is an intergovernmental body which meets in full session in Geneva once a year (usually in October). In addition to the 51 member states, non-member states, representatives from non-governmental organizations and intergovernmental organizations also attend as observers. At this meeting, EXCOM makes decisions, called Conclusions, on specific aspects of refugee protection that are intended to guide UNHCR and specify actions on behalf of refugees.

Conclusions are not legally binding on states in the same sense as treaties; however, as most are adopted by consensus by over 40 states, they represent the views of the international community and carry persuasive authority. They have covered numerous issues, including:

- EXCOM Conclusion 6: principle of *non-refoulement*
- EXCOM Conclusion 8: determination of refugee status
- EXCOM Conclusion 22: protection of asylum-seekers in situation of large-scale influx
- EXCOM Conclusion 30: the problem of manifestly

    unfounded or abusive application for refugee status
or asylum
- EXCOM Conclusion 44: detention of refugees and asylum-seekers
- EXCOM Conclusion 59: special needs of refugee children
- EXCOM Conclusion 64: specific needs of refugee women
- EXCOM Conclusion 73: refugee protection and sexual violence
- EXCOM Conclusion 75: internally displaced persons

ENDNOTES

[1] For Amnesty International, prisoners of conscience are people detained anywhere for their beliefs or because of their ethnic origin, sex, colour, language, national or social origin, economic status, birth or other status — who have not used or advocated violence.

[2] For a general discussion of *"non-entrée"*, see J.C. Hathaway, "Can International Refugee Law Be Made Relevant Again?", in *World Refugee Survey 1996*, US Refugee Committee.

[3] *UNHCR: The State of the World's Refugees 1995.*

[4] Article 1 A 2. These criteria are known as the "material nature" of the refugee definition.

[5] See generally for a discussion of refugees and international law, Guy S. Goodwin-Gill, *The Refugee in International Law*, 1996 and J. C. Hathaway, *The Law of Refugee Status*, 1991.

[6] Article I.2. The OAU Convention entered into force on 20 June 1974.

[7] Annual Report of the Inter-American Commission on Human Rights, 1984-85. The Cartagena Declaration was approved by the OAS General Assembly in 1985.

[8] For a discussion of the UNHCR view of refugees and "people of concern" see V. Turk, "The Role of the United Nations High Commissioner for Refugees (UNHCR) in the Development of International Refugee Law", *Proceedings of the Conference on Refugee Rights and Realities*, University of Nottingham, November 1996.

[9] UN General Assembly Resolution 2312 (XXII).

[10] Article 1 (3) of the UN Declaration on Territorial Asylum: "It shall rest with the State granting asylum to evaluate the grounds for the grant of asylum."

[11] EXCOM Conclusions 6 and 22.

[12] Recommendation R (84) 1 on the Protection of Persons Satisfying the Criteria in the Geneva Convention who are not Formally Recognised as Refugees, adopted by the Committee of Ministers of the Council of Europe on 25 January 1984.

[13] *Chahal v. United Kingdom*, judgment of 15 November 1996.

[14] P. Weis, *The Refugee Convention*, 1951, Cambridge 1995, Commentary to Article 31, 303.

[15] EXCOM Conclusion 15 provides at (i): "While asylum-seekers may be required to submit their asylum request within a certain time limit, failure to do so, or the non-fulfilment of other formal requirements, should not lead to an asylum request being excluded from consideration."

[16] UN Refugee Convention, Article 31 (2).

[17] In the Conference of Plenipotentiaries Final Act, family unity is identified as an "essential right". However, the UN Refugee Convention is silent on the issue. The Convention on the Rights of the Child provides that states should expedite the reunion of the child and the family, but there is no right to family unity *per se*.

[18] See also EXCOM Conclusion 39 "Refugee Women and International Protection", 1985, and Conclusion 73 "Refugee Protection and Sexual Violence", 1993.

[19] See also Article 22 regarding measures a state shall take for children seeking

refugee status and family reunification.

[20] France and Italy, which had made the declaration in 1954, both subsequently extended their obligations to refugees from "Europe or elsewhere", France in 1971 and Italy in 1990.

[21] Congo removed the limitation in 1970.

[22] Article 1 (3) of the 1967 Protocol. See also Amnesty International's report: *Turkey — Selective protection: Discriminatory treatment of non-European refugees and asylum-seekers* (AI Index: EUR 44/16/94).

[23] *Sales, Acting Commissioner, INS v. Haitian Centers Council,* 113 S. Ct 2549 (1993).

[24] Resolution on the Harmonization within the European Community of asylum law and policies, Resolution A3-0337/92 of 18 November 1992; this position was repeated in slightly altered wording by the European Parliament in its resolution A3-0404/93 of 19 January 1994.

[25] UN Refugee Convention, Article 31.

[26] UNHCR, *Detention of Asylum-Seekers in Europe,* 1995, p. 57. The analysis was based on responses to a questionnaire from UNHCR local offices — not all responded on the issue of penalties for illegal entry.

[27] EXCOM Conclusions 8 and 15 (j).

[28] Council of Europe Recommendation 3.

[29] EXCOM Conclusion 44.

[30] EXCOM Conclusion 44 (b).

[31] A letter from UNHCR (signed by Ghassan Arnaout, Division of Refugee Law and Doctrine) to the European Consultation on Refugees and Exiles of 8 January 1987 states that this criterion "means that a person may, if necessary, be detained to undergo a preliminary interview. It does not justify the detention of a person for the entire duration of a prolonged asylum procedure."

[32] In the same 8 January 1987 letter, UNHCR states:"There must furthermore be an intention to mislead the authorities. Thus an asylum seeker who arrives without documentation ... cannot be detained under this specific heading. Similarly an asylum seeker who has destroyed his documents ... but informs the authorities of his identity, the elements of his claim, and his travels, should not be detained under this heading."

[33] Each detainee must be informed promptly of the right to a lawyer of his/her own choice and how to avail him/herself of this right (UN Body of Principles 13). The detainee has the right to communicate with and be visited by counsel without delay. The detainee and his/her counsel must have adequate time and facilities for the preparation of their case concerning the lawfulness of detention (UN Body of Principles 17,18).

[34] EXCOM Conclusion 44 (g) and 22.III.

[35] UN Body of Principles for the Protection of All Persons under Any Form of Detention or Imprisonment (UN Body of Principles) 16; UN Standard Minimum Rules for the Treatment of Prisoners 92.

[36] UN Body of Principles 19; UN Standard Minimum Rules for the Treatment of Prisoners 92.

[37] UN Body of Principles 19.

[38] UN Body of Principles 24, 25 and 26.

[39] EXCOM Conclusion 44(f).

[40] 1989 Convention on the Rights of the Child, Article 37.

[41] UNHCR Handbook para 203.

[42] The Schengen Supplementary Agreement ("Convention applying the Schengen Agreement of 14 June 1985") was signed by an initial group of five EU member states (Benelux countries, Germany and France) in June 1990. Further EU member states joined and it entered into force on 26 April 1995.

The Dublin Convention on determining the state responsible for examining applications for asylum lodged in one of the member states of the European Communities, signed by 11 ministers responsible for immigration in June 1990. The (then) 12th Member State, Denmark, signed in 1991.

[43] This contravenes EXCOM Conclusion 12 of October 1978, which states "... a decision by a Contracting State (of the 1951 Convention and the 1967 Protocol) not to recognize refugee status does not preclude another Contracting State from examining a new request for refugee status made by the person concerned."

[44] The Comprehensive Plan of Action was introduced in 1989 as a measure to address the problem of countries of first refuge refusing to allow asylum-seekers to settle locally. Thousands of refugees rescued at sea were not allowed to disembark and seek protection in countries in the region.

[45] UNHCR Information Note, "Temporary Protection", para 11, 20 April 1995.

[46] EXCOM Conclusion 65.

[47] See Amnesty International, *Bosnia-Herzegovina: "Who's living in my house?" Obstacles to the safe return of refugees and displaced people* (AI Index: EUR 63/01/97), 1997.

[48] A host state may end the protection given to a refugee by invoking the "cessation clauses" of the UN Refugee Convention. These clauses apply when a refugee can once again rely on the protection of their own state or when the reasons for flight no longer exist, so that the refugee can return home in safety. A state may only invoke these clauses if there is evidence of a change in circumstances that is effective and of an enduring nature. Also, a refugee must have an opportunity to show why the effects of past persecution may be so traumatizing that they cannot return to their country of origin. (See UN Refugee Convention, Article 1C.)

[49] In 1994 UNHCR stated that a declaration of guiding principles would appear to be a desirable and feasible option for providing assistance to refugees from armed conflict. Para 54, Note on International Protection, submitted by the High Commissioner for Refugees to EXCOM A/AC.96/830, 7 September 1994.

[50] *Op cit.*, para 63.

[51] *Ibid.*

[52] Para 14, Note on International Protection, submitted by the High Commissioner for Refugees to EXCOM A/AC.96/850, 1 September 1995.

[53] Para 35, Summary Record of the 504th Meeting, EXCOM (General Debate) A/AC.96/SR.504.